SATAN IS NO MYTH

SATAN IS NO MYTH

J. OSWALD SANDERS

MOODY PRESS
CHICAGO

Library of Congress Cataloging in Publication Data

Sanders, John Oswald, 1902-
 Satan is no myth.
 1. Devil.   I. Title.
BT981.S26   235'.47   74-15358
ISBN 0-8024-7525-6

3 4 5 6 7 Printing/GB/Year 87 86 85 84 83 82

Printed in the United States of America

Contents

Preface

THE CONSISTENT THEME OF THE BIBLE from beginning to end is the conflict between good and evil, between God and the devil. It begins with the serpent in Eden in Genesis 3 and concludes with the devil cast into the lake of fire in Revelation 20. The intervening chapters depict the swaying tides of battle in a conflict waged in the heavenly sphere as well as on earth.

Since that is so, is it not both strange and suspicious that there is so little literature dealing specifically with the devil, who, according to Scripture, is the second most powerful being in the universe? Is it not surprising that this theme is so seldom the subject of preaching in our churches? I have often questioned people on this subject, only to discover that a good proportion have never heard even one sermon on the devil and his activities. The reader need only consult his own experience to realize how singularly successful the devil has been in disguising his activities and preserving his anonymity.

The reason for this singular neglect is not because of a lack of material on the subject in the Scriptures. Indeed, there is an amazing amount of teaching to throw light on every aspect of Satan's person and work. And it is not because there is not adequate and tragic evidence of his nefarious activity that can be seen by the discerning eye.

We must look elsewhere for the reason for that strange omission.

Satan is no myth. It would be difficult to refute Beaudelaire's contention that the devil's cleverest ruse is to make men believe that he does not exist. The immediate result of the church's neglect has been the large number swept into the vortex of the occult revival. And few voices are raised to alert people to the significance of this revival.

1

Myth or Reality?

In the desperate conflict Christ waged, in which He lost His life, was He mistaken? Was it really 'the prince of this world' He had to face—a terrible supernatural being whose hate for God was as dark and as deep as hell? Or was He deluded?

That He believed in a personal devil whose dominion He came to shatter; that He commanded demons to come out of their victims; that He was convinced that if He were to save man He must show up the Prince of Darkness in his true light, and break his power over human hearts; that He really believed these things, no student of the Scriptures would for a moment pretend to deny.[1]

F. J. Huegel

NOTE SOME STATEMENTS that are a fair representation of a very large cross-section of theological opinion in our day:

No present-day system of philosophy gives any place to the Diabolos of Scripture.[2]

Edgar Brightman

The toothy red imp with tail and trident has become a secular figure of fun, and many theologians have banished a personal devil to the realm of myth.[3]

J. I. Packer

Until the Age of Enlightenment (A.D. 1650-1780) be-

9

lief in an objectivised personal devil and his minions was all but universal amongst theologians. Today, however, it is generally recognized that belief in Satan, the leader of the fallen angels, etc., is not a satisfactory answer to the problem of evil. It still leaves us to ask the question how evil got into the world which God created and saw was "very good." But as a pictorial way of representing the existence of superhuman evil forces in the universe, Satan and his hosts call our attention to a very important question for theology.[4]

Alan Richardson

Reasons for those attitudes are many. First and foremost, perhaps, are the grotesque, fantastic representations of the devil, which in the past travestied the sober and restrained language of Scripture. Popular conceptions are based more on the word pictures of Dante and Milton than on divine revelation.

The medieval picture of a half-man, half-beast with horns, cloven hoofs, and tail, is a masterly gambit of the devil to make himself appear so ludicrous as to get himself laughed out of court. No being could be less like "the anointed cherub," "the angel of light" who is next to Christ in power and worldly authority. Ebrard maintained that all the objections raised by philosophers are not against the devil as portrayed in the Bible, but against false conceptions of him invented in the past and perpetuated in modern literature.

Owen C. Whitehouse, an avowedly advanced biblical critic, concludes his article in *Hastings' Dictionary of the Bible* with: "That Satan exists as a personal center of evil influences, physical as well as moral (for the two are closely associated), is the undoubted teaching of the Bible."[5] That being the case, the concept of a personal devil is rejected only on the a priori grounds that it is too grotesque for refined minds to accept, or that it does not supply the whole answer to the problem of evil.

The Only Authentic Source

The only authentic source of knowledge of the realm of the unseen is the divine revelation of the Scriptures. All else is speculation, with no one view more authoritative than another. Where Scripture is silent, or speaks with reserve, the expositor will do well to advance only tentative opinions. But where Scripture has spoken clearly, we have heard all we need to know, and our opinions need not be tentative.

The Bible reveals truths that intellectual research or psychic investigation have never revealed. A. T. Pierson wrote:

> One of the grand proofs that the Scriptures are God-inspired is found in the air of absolute positiveness and infallible certainty with which these occult mysteries are treated. There is no timid feeling after truth, or hesitating utterance about it, but a consistent body of teaching concerning the unseen realm, that has at least this to commend it, for the first and only time, it gives man a simple and satisfactory solution of perhaps his greatest problem. Here is teaching that has about it *finality;* it is the utterance of One who speaks as confidently as about the most common facts or phenomena, and treats what is hidden from the senses as a familiar commonplace. He who after vain attempts to find in man's hypotheses and philosophies any solid ground to rest upon, comes with open mind and heart to inquire at God's living oracles, gets an answer to all his inquiries and a sure basis for faith and hope.[6]

His contention was that, to the believer, the realm of the unseen is an indisputable reality whose existence and importance are never argued in Scripture, but assumed.

Referring to the growing disbelief in a personal devil among theologians, Maldwyn Hughes says:

> Many theologians are opposed to it on the ground that it introduces an ultimate dualism into the universe. But this is not so unless the Divine attributes of omniscience, omnipotence and omnipresence are ascribed to Satan. The existence of a demonic intelligence no more necessarily implies dualism than does the existence of sinful man. Without seeking to dogmatize, it may be remarked that belief in the diabolic personality rests on the same general ground of experience as belief in the divine personality. But since the latter belief is comforting and the former belief disturbing, people overlook the parallelism.[7]

THE DEVIL'S INCOGNITO

The very names applied to Satan by our Lord argue his personality. Murder is not a mere abstraction and does not exist apart from a murderer. There is no lie without a liar (John 8:44). In the Bible, moral evil is uniformly viewed as the product of personality. It exists only in the wills of personal beings, whether human or superhuman. To think otherwise is not rational.

The devil's incognito is one of the cleverest tricks in his bag. Denis de Rougemont writes in *La Part du Diable:*

> But the devil, who is possessed with desire to imitate truth in twisting it, says to us, "I am nobody. What are you afraid of? Are you going to tremble before the nonexistent?" . . . Satan disappears in his successes and his triumph is his incognito. The proof that the devil exists, acts, and succeeds lies in the fact that the intelligent world does not believe in him any more.[8]

THE KEY QUESTION

To one who believes Christ to be the Son of God in the fullest sense of that term, and who accepts the Scriptures as the inspired and authoritative revelation of God, one key question bears on the subject of the reality of the devil and his demons. That question is, *"Did Jesus believe in the existence of a personal devil and his demons, or was His conception of only impersonal but powerful forces of evil in the universe?"* The way we answer that question will determine our whole approach to the subject. If our Lord disbelieved the existence of a personal, malignant devil, then we need not hesitate to share His disbelief.

If our Lord's words on the subject are taken objectively, the conclusion, whether He was right or wrong, is that He believed and taught that He engaged in conflict with a personal tempter in the wilderness temptation. The language carries no other construction. He spoke and acted as though there was a personal devil, whose dominion over men He had come to shatter, whose power He had come to render inoperative. He claimed that on His cross sentence was passed on "the ruler of this world" and that his doom is sure.

Some have pointed out that in the parable of the sower Jesus interpreted His teaching as referring not to impersonal evil but to a personal *evil one* (Matthew 13:19). If Jesus had only impersonal evil in mind, His words would be devoid of meaning.

Three views have been advanced to explain Christ's apparent belief in a personal devil and attendant evil spirits:

1. Our Lord, living in a primitive and unscientific age, shared with those of His own day a superstitious

belief in a personal devil, but both He and they were mistaken. He had been granted only the degree of knowledge essential to His mission to earth. In other matters He shared the errors and superstitious beliefs of His age.

2. Jesus did not share those mistaken beliefs, but He accommodated His speech and actions to what was generally believed in His day. His mission was to teach spiritual truths, not science, and He did that in the language of the people. This argument has been stated more subtly: There can be no doubt, it runs, that Jesus spoke as though Satan was a reality, but it is open to argument that He was simply using the thought forms of His age, without making any pronouncement on their truth or otherwise.

3. He believed in the existence of a personal devil, and in this He was correct.

The first suggested explanation, which represents Christ as sharing the errors and superstitions of His day, strikes a direct blow at His omniscience. It involves a denial of His claim to a knowledge of the unseen world from which He claimed to have come and also impugns the integrity of Scripture.

The second suggested explanation involves even more serious factors. It would show Jesus to be not only less than ingenuous, but also positively untruthful, for He purposely conveyed an impression contrary to the truth. It represents Him not as instructing but as deceiving His disciples, as encouraging superstition rather than teaching truth. It presents Him in a light entirely inconsistent with His claim to be a teacher sent from God, since it represents Him as personifying diseases and actually addressing them as demons. But most incredible of all, it represents Him as making use of an unfounded superstition to substantiate His claim to divine authority, since His delegation to His disciples of power to cast out demons was regarded as a divine attestation of His mission.

Consider the implications of the first two suggested explanations. If either is true, we are left with a sinful man, less than God, and of limited intelligence—the exact reverse of the picture of Him the gospels uniformly portray. Further, the foundations of our confidence in Him as Savior and Lord are shattered. If we cannot place confidence in His teaching on this point, what grounds do we have to believe His teaching about God the Father and salvation? If He equivocated in what He taught about Satan, how can we be sure that He was not equivocating when He spoke about God?

True, He clothed His teaching in striking figures and picturesque language, but He did not use those figures and language to convey concepts that were the opposite of truth. He who *is* the Truth could not and would not speak anything but absolute truth. If He did, He was not the sinless Son of God.

We are left with the third explanation. Jesus did believe in the existence of a personal devil and attendant evil spirits, and His belief was grounded in fact.

2

Origin and Fall

*God is absolute Good, and only Good. Nothing that is
not good could come from such a Source. A sweet
fountain may send forth poison; the sun may produce
darkness and night sooner than God produce evil in
the sense of wickedness. He therefore no more created
the devil as such, that is as he now is, than He created
man as he now is. No "liar" or "murderer" ever sprang
from His creative will.[1]*

F. C. Jennings

IN HIS INSCRUTABLE WISDOM, God ordained that Scripture
should have little to say concerning the origin and apostasy of the devil. We are given a number of hints and
clues but few categorical statements. Two passages of
Scripture appear to have bearing upon this subject; but
we must acknowledge that views on their correct interpretation are strongly polarized.

One school of thought holds that Isaiah 14:4-21 and
Ezekiel 28:12-19 refer solely to the earthly kings of
Babylon or Tyre, who are the human subjects of the
prophecies, with no further application. Both kings
were rich and notoriously arrogant, and both were
stripped of their power and brought low because of
their pride, as the prophets foretold.

No explicit reference is made to Satan in either passage, it is said, and it is unwarranted spiritualizing and false exegesis to suggest he is in view even in a secondary sense. This position is held by some evangelical expositors as well as by those who do not accept the factuality of a personal devil and demons.

The other school of thought, which includes many reputable theologians, maintains that those prophetic passages give valuable insight into Satan's original state and the sin that led to his downfall. Both schools can produce strong arguments in support of their own positions.

Both parties concede that the *primary* reference of both passages was to the earthly kings of Babylon and Tyre, and that there is no *direct* reference to Satan's origin and fall. Also, they concede it is a questionable practice to base important doctrinal conclusions on pictorial and poetic passages of Scripture. If, however, there are other reasonable grounds for such an assumption that in no way contravene the tenor of Scripture, then we should be ready to consider the case for it.

"There is a latent mystic significance in these passages, interwoven with their more immediate reference to local and historical persons and happenings." That statement summarizes the second view. Even before the Christian era, Jewish expositors assumed that Satan was the one addressed. As early as the third century, some of the early church Fathers interpreted both passages as ultimate references to the fall of Satan. So the second view is by no means a modern innovation.

The following considerations are advanced as reasons that would support the second view:

1. *Some of the expressions used could not under any circumstances be applied to a mere human king.* Of what heathen king could it conceivably be said,

"You had the seal of perfection, full of wisdom and perfect in beauty. You were in Eden, the garden of God; every precious stone was your covering: . . . You were on the holy mountain of God; . . . You were blameless in your ways from the day you were created, until unrighteousness was found in you" (Ezekiel 28:12-15).

Since those are the words of the Lord God (28:11), who is guilty of neither equivocation nor exaggeration, they must be given their full value. In what conceivable sense could those words apply to any king of Tyre of which we have knowledge? Taken even in a poetic sense, the statements imply an original perfection and presaged a subsequent disastrous fall that could be found in no heathen king.

2. *There is frequently a double fulfilment in biblical prophecy*—one immediate and one more remote. In His guidance of His prophets, God often enabled them to see events far beyond their own times and to make pronouncements that envisaged powerful spiritual forces behind what seemed to be purely temporal happenings. "The prophets who prophesied of the grace that would come to you made careful search and inquiry, seeking to know what person or time the Spirit of Christ within them was indicating as He predicted the sufferings of Christ and the glories to follow. It was revealed to them that they were not serving themselves but you" (1 Peter 1:10-12).

The prophetic writings begin with normal human experience but frequently go beyond man to one who is much more than man.

3. *A study of the messianic prophecies reveals just such a pattern.* Old Testament passages that foreshadow the Messiah, and are attested as such in the

New Testament, usually sprang from very ordinary circumstances. For example, which of us would have discerned in the incident of the serpent of brass the application our Lord gave it? Compare Numbers 21:9 with John 3:14; also Isaiah 7:10-14 with Matthew 1:23.

Some of David's experiences recounted in the Psalms were genuine personal experiences, but they are described in language that obviously had a deeper significance and a wider application. Many such statements are later, in the New Testament, related to the experiences of the Messiah. Psalm 22 is a notable example of this method of revelation. While speaking of himself, David, under the inspiration of the Holy Spirit, made statements and described conditions that could find their fulfilment only in the Messiah.

If David's personal experience could thus be intertwined with that of his Greater Son, is it unreasonable to suggest that God may have adopted a similar method to shed light on the original perfection and subsequent degradation of His archrival? Why should He not inspire those poetic descriptions to afford us a glimpse of the devil's former glory and an explanation of his formidable powers?

4. Scripture assigns to Satan a position of great power and authority in the present world-system, for example, "The god of this world has blinded the minds of the unbelieving, that they might not see the light of the gospel" (2 Corinthians 4:4). Bearing that in mind, is it unreasonable to assume that God here enabled the prophets to see beyond the earthly realm of evil the activity of the supremely evil spirit who controls and inspires it?

Is it inconceivable that behind the forces of human history there is a kingdom of evil—that beyond and behind the kings of Tyre and Babylon the prophets saw in vision the sinister evil one who used those kings as instruments?

5. What could more appropriately foreshadow and represent the prince of this age than the head of the greatest atheistic world power, Babylon?

6. Even allowing the words of Isaiah 14:13-14 as poetical, would they not be absurd on the lips of a heathen king? But they would not be inappropriate from the powerful and ambitious evil spirit who controlled the king of Babylon.

7. If this suggested interpretation of these passages is *not* acceptable, would we not be left in the dark concerning the entrance of sin into the universe, and with little information concerning the history and ambitions of the enemy of God and man? But if these passages *are* accepted as having such implications, large tracts of Scripture are illumined, and we gain insight into the devil's aims and strategy.

8. We submit that the suggested interpretation in no way contradicts, but is entirely consistent with, the remainder of the teaching of Scripture concerning the devil and his followers.

So although it is not dogmatically claimed that the above is the authoritative interpretation of Isaiah 14 and Ezekiel 28, there appear to be stronger reasons to accept than to reject it. Those reasons are summarized as follows: (a) It is consistent with the tenor of Scripture; (b) it is consistent with the method of interpretation applied to other prophetic Scriptures; (c) it is not absurd like much ancient myth and tradition, but is restrained and credible; (d) it helps to discredit the grotesque representations of the devil that have served him so well, in making him the object of ridicule and discounting the reality of his existence; (e) it throws light on the unseen realm that is given nowhere else.

WHAT ARE THE LESSONS?

1. Satan is represented as a created being, neither self-existent nor self-sufficient (Ezekiel 28:13,15). He was a free moral agent, capable of choosing good or evil.
2. Like all God's creation, he left God's hand perfect and not as a foul fiend (28:12,15).
3. He was invested with great wisdom and beauty (28:12).
4. His defection would appear to be the beginning of sin in the universe (28:15).
5. He cherished unholy ambition and his heart was lifted up with pride. "I will raise my throne above the stars of God, . . . I will make myself like the Most High" (Isaiah 14:13-14). Speaking of Satan and those spirits whom he drew away with him, Augustine wrote: "Bartering the lofty dignity of eternity for the inflation of pride, trading the most assured verity for the slyness of vanity, they became proud, deceived, envious."
6. He became an essentially selfish being, infatuated with himself, and endeavoring to usurp the prerogatives of God (Isaiah 14:13).
7. The sentence of expulsion was pronounced on him (Ezekiel 28:16).
8. The ignominious fall of the earthly kings and kingdoms of Babylon and Tyre prefigure the fall of the ruler and the kingdom of darkness.
9. The essence of Lucifer's sin is seen in the fivefold "I

will" (Isaiah 14:13-14). Not satisfied with delegated authority, he aspired to enjoy unbridled license. He was not under the pressure of necessity to sin, but chose it of his own volition. It was true of him as Milton wrote of Adam:

> No decree of God
> Concurring to necessitate his fall,
> Or touch with lightest moment of impulse
> His free Will, to her own inclining left
> In even scale.

One of the oldest books of the Bible is the book of Job, and it affords further light on Satan's early activities in the world. Satan is presented in its early chapters as one whom someone has called "the supreme cynic of the heavenly court." His name is mentioned for the first time in the Old Testament in Job 1:8, where he appears with "the sons of God" (angels) before the Lord. From this we learn that, despite his fall, he still had right of access into God's presence. But it is clear that he came before God in no reverent spirit but with a sinister truculence.

Unknown to the man Job, whom God described as "a blameless and an upright man," Job became a battle-ground for a test of strength between God and Satan. The devil's cynical question, "Does Job fear God for nought?" was throwing down the gauntlet, and the challenge was accepted by God (1:12). Satan sneeringly suggested that Job's loyalty to God was far from being disinterested. God had "bought" it by His preferential treatment. "Does Job fear God for nought?" God staked everything on the fidelity of His servant, and He was not disappointed. Through devastating reverses and desperate suffering, Job maintained his integrity and loyalty to God and refused to be lured from the heights of faith. Satan retired from the field vanquished. Job demonstrated that his love and loyalty to God were indeed disinterested.

Several important truths emerge from this account: Although Satan's powers are definitely under divine control and he cannot exceed the limits of divine permission, God has allowed him great powers. He could incite the Sabeans to attack and kill Job's children and the Chaldeans to kill his cattle and servants (1:15,17). He had power to cause lightning to come from heaven and to originate a cyclone (1:16,19). He had the power to afflict Job with bodily disease (2:7). He confessed that his occupation was "roaming about on the earth and walking around on it" (1:7). The significance of that expression is "going to and fro *as a spy*." He spies on men with the evil purpose of accusing them.

Thus, early in human history—for Job was possibly a contemporary of Abraham—God gave His people some insight into what transpires in the realm of the unseen and some idea of the tactics of their enemy.

3

Names and Nature

As Satan, the opposer of blessing to man, we see him in many passages of the Old Testament. Yet so apparently righteous are his pleas, so well-founded in the evident guilt of the accused, that many commentators emphatically assert that the Satan of the Old Testament is really a kind of spiritual attorney-general to prosecute evil wherever found . . . His full, true character is only revealed, his full, true name only told us when the Lord Jesus comes in the flesh, and he attacks Him. Then for the first time he is plainly called the devil.[1]

F. C. Jennings

TO PEOPLE OF THE WESTERN WORLD, names have little more than a sentimental significance. But it was, and is, far different in Eastern lands, and especially in Bible times. To those people names were descriptive and significant.

Sometimes they were the expression of the faith of the child's parents, as with Elijah, whose name means *Jehovah is my God.* Jacob's name was changed from *cheat, supplanter* to *Israel,* which means *a prince with God.* Sometimes the name described physical characteristics, as with Esau, whose name means *red,* and Laban, *blond.*

Among the means of God's self-revelation to His creatures are the names used of Him. A surprising variety of names and titles are ascribed to and used of the members

24

of the Trinity. In his book *The Wonderful Names of Our Wonderful Lord,* T. C. Horton lists no fewer than 365. Each name reveals a fresh facet of God's character or of His relations with men. His revelation of Himself through His names is progressive and cumulative, and gradually unfolds His personality, character, and attributes.

In the same way, the nature, character, and activities of the devil progressively unfold in the names and titles used of him. At least thirty different names describe his person and delineate his work. It is significant that his full name and nature were revealed only when Jesus came and smoked him out into the open. In the Old Testament he is only a shadowy figure.

An examination of Satan's more prominent names will greatly illuminate our study:

SATAN

"Satan" means *adversary, opposer,* and is mentioned as many times in the Bible as the names of all the other angels put together. It is used of human adversaries, for example, 1 Kings 11:14, 23. But the Hebrews uniformly reserved it for the devil. In fifty-six instances, he is invariably represented as the implacable adversary of God and man. In Job he is the prosecuting counsel, bringing charge against God's loyal servant Job.

He is seen, too, in the role of hinderer of the purposes of God. "For we wanted to come to you—I, Paul, more than once—and yet Satan thwarted us" (1 Thessalonians 2:18). He is uniformly regarded as a malignant, malicious personality, hostile to God and man, working to thwart the Lord's beneficent purposes.

THE DEVIL

The Hebrew word often translated *devil* literally

means "hairy" and is used of a goat or satyr (Isaiah 13:21; 34:14). Could that be the basis of the common conception of the devil as a hairy being with horns and hoofs? Satyrs were conceived of as demon spirits who inhabited the desert and who had to be appeased by sacrifice. The word is always used with an evil connotation.

The Greek term *diabolos* has the meaning of "slanderer, traducer, malignant accuser," and is used thirty-five times in the New Testament. It was the term applied to a paid informer. It was the devil who tempted Jesus in the wilderness. In Eden he slandered God to Eve, impugning His integrity and casting doubt on the reality of His love. He slandered Job to God, alleging that his professed loyalty to God, far from being genuine, spontaneous, and disinterested, had been bought by God through preferential treatment.

The devil is never better pleased than when he can reproduce his own characteristics in the child of God by influencing one Christian to slander another. Nothing breaks the unity of the Spirit like this subtle and sinister tactic of the enemy, and nothing should be more abjured by the Christian.

BEELZEBUB

In the Old Testament, Baal-zebub appears as the god of the Philistines of Kron. It was this god whom King Ahaziah sought to consult (2 Kings 1:2,16). He reappears in the New Testament as Beelzebub, described as "the ruler of demons" (Matthew 12:24).

The names means "lord of flies," a concept that has caused him to be termed "the genius who presides over corruption," an apt description of one of Satan's major activities.

The devil corrupts everything he touches. He corrupts *personal life* by encouraging "the new morality," falsely so-called. He corrupts *social life* by inciting men and women to drunkenness, debauchery, and drugs. He corrupts *political life* through bribery and insincerity. He corrupts *Christian doctrine* by introducing "doctrines of demons." His corrupting influence invades all human thought and action.

In the light of that, we are in a position to evaluate the seriousness and blasphemy of the charge laid against Jesus—that He exorcised demons by the power of Beelzebub, for Jesus identified Beelzebub with Satan (12:26). We also have, in this name, some insight into the nature of "the sin that never has forgiveness" (Mark 3:29).

THE SERPENT

"That serpent of old who is called the devil and Satan" is the way he is described in Revelation 12:9. Isaiah called him "Leviathan, the fleeing serpent . . . the twisted serpent" (Isaiah 27:1). Jesus Himself used the serpent as the symbol of deceit and hypocrisy (Matthew 23:33), and Paul gave it a similar connotation: "But I am afraid, lest as the serpent deceived Eve by his craftiness, your minds should be led astray from the simplicity and purity of devotion to Christ" (2 Corinthians 11:3).

The one who is later identified as the devil appeared first on the pages of Scripture under this name in Genesis 3:1: "Now the serpent was more crafty than any beast of the field." The word for "crafty" is translated *prudent* in Proverbs 22:3. The consummate wisdom with which Satan was apparently endowed before his fall degenerated into craftiness and evil cunning.

The Hebrew word for serpent, *nachash,* may mean "to hiss or to shine," and so could represent him as "the bright, the shining one." That would account for the fact that Eve was not repelled by his approach. In the ancient world, and also in our modern sophisticated world, the serpent was regarded as an object of worship. Whatever the nature of the creature who was possessed by the devil, it was so attractive, and its approach so natural, that is aroused neither fear nor suspicion in Eve—and thus more easily accomplished her downfall.

MURDERER

None other than our Lord Himself invested the devil with the title *murderer.* "You are of your father the devil," He said to the Jews, "and you want to do the desires of your father. *He was a murderer from the beginning,* and does not stand in the truth, because there is no truth in him" (John 8:44, italics added).

"You seek to kill Me," Jesus charged them. "You also do the things which you heard from your father" (John 8:37-38).

From the dawn of history Satan has manifested a passion to kill and destroy. Our Lord confirmed that devilish characteristic in the pungent words of His parable: "The thief comes only to steal, and kill, and destroy" (John 10:10).

The devil showed his hand in the primal family, when the first fratricide was perpetrated. Since that tragedy, murder has been endemic in the human race. The fact that this crime has reached such tremendous proportions is clear evidence of the accelerated activity of Satan at the end of the age. In one week, when I was in Manila, no fewer than forty-nine murders were reported in that city. Scripture asserts that Satan will pursue his murderous course right up to the very gates of heaven (Revelation 7:14).

THE ROARING LION

It is characteristic of the lion that it stalks its prey both stealthily and ruthlessly. So, says Peter, "Your adversary, the devil, prowls about like *a roaring lion,* seeking someone to devour" (1 Peter 5:8, italics added). Like the lion, too, his purpose is always destruction. He never gives advance notice of his intentions, nor does he betray his presence until he is ready to strike. He roars *after* the kill, not before.

In this guise, the adversary strikes terror into the hearts of his victims. How tragically he succeeds among those in the grip of animism! In this character he launches his blitzkriegs of persecution on many new churches and believers. The Toradja Church in Sulawesi, Indonesia, suffered terrible persecution from its fanatical Muslim neighbors. Christians were crucified, sewn in the skins of animals, and cast into the river. In spite of the worst the "lion" could do, the church not only stood firm but also grew.

No individual or church or missionary society is exempt from satanic attentions. He is constantly on the prowl—hence Peter's counsel, "Be of sober spirit, be on the alert." He has been well called "Sabbathless Satan," for he is never off duty.

But he skillfully adapts his tactics to suit the prey he pursues. To the raw pagan, his most effective role may be that of a roaring lion. To the sophisticated philosopher, he will more likely transform himself into an angel of light. "Even Satan disguises himself as an angel of light" (2 Corinthians 11:14).

LIAR

Satan can speak the truth, but our Lord implied that he was a liar even when he spoke the truth! If he does speak truth, it is for no good purpose. All that he does is false, evil, sinister. "He has nothing to do with the truth," Jesus said, "because there is no truth in him. When he lies, he speaks according to his own nature, for *he is a liar* and the father of lies" (John 8:44, RSV,* italics added).

Satan is the fountain and focal point of all falsehood, deceit, and trickery in the world. While he poses at times as the champion of divine law, he is all the time undermining it. He falsifies truth, misrepresents it, twists it, mixes it with error. And he does it so skillfully as to deceive the very elect. As the father of lies, he fosters and encourages hypocrisy, exaggeration, and deceit.

THE TEMPTER

The term *tempter* is used twice in the New Testament. In the wilderness temptation of our Lord, *"The tempter* came and said to Him . . . (Matthew 4:3, italics added). Paul employs it, too. "I sent to find out about your faith, for fear that *the tempter* might have tempted you, and our labor should be in vain" (1 Thessalonians 3:5, italics added).

The verb *to tempt* has two senses in Scripture. One is neutral and means simply "to test," as in assaying and refining gold. The other means to tempt in the sense of "inciting to evil."

Trial and temptation are sometimes matters in which both God and Satan are involved. The same event may be both a test and a temptation to evil, as in the case of

Revised Standard Version.

Joseph's temptation by Potiphar's wife. The man of God can expect both experiences. Satan's objective is to encompass our ruin. God's aim is to establish us in holiness, for God incites no one to evil (James 1:13).

Bishop Moule has pointed out there are two parallel Hebrew and Greek words used to differentiate the two ideas. One pair means "to test with a view to separating the gold from the dross." Always used in a good sense, they denote tests and trials sent from God.

The other pair signifies "to prove with a view to finding and exploiting the weak spot," as in a military campaign. The objective is usually evil—always so when relating to Satan.

The devil has no greater desire than to tempt and incite to sin. He did that with the celestial spirits who are called "his angels," and caused them to "lose their first estate" (Matthew 12:24; Jude 6; Revelation 12:7). He aimed to frustrate God's purposes of grace for mankind by tempting them to abandon loyal obedience to God. "The artistry of the devil is to make himself invisible in our temptations."

THE DRAGON

The title *dragon* as applied to Satan is found in the New Testament only in the Revelation. "Behold, a *great red dragon*. . . . And there was war in heaven, Michael and his angels waging war with the dragon. And the dragon and his angels waged war, and they were not strong enough" (Revelation 12:3, 7-8, italics added).

The word was used of any great monster of the land or sea, and here applies to an apocalyptic monster. To the Greeks, the dragon was a fabulous and mythical creature, ferocious and frightening, and possessed of dread malignant power. In the passage before us, the dragon is implacably set on the destruction of God's people (12:4) and is identified with "the devil and Satan" (12:9).

THE EVIL ONE

Just as God is the embodiment of all that is good and holy, so the devil is the embodiment of all that is evil and unholy. In him evil reaches its nadir. His influence for evil is all-pervasive. "We know that . . . the whole world lies in the power of the evil one," wrote John (1 John 5:19). The picture is of one lying unconscious in his arms.

THE ACCUSER OF THE BRETHREN

Ernest Renan described Satan as "the malevolent critic of creation." Here is another sinister aspect of the devil's unceasing warfare against the Christian who desires to walk closely with God.

He who is the father of lies can speak the truth when it suits him. No matter whether they are false or true, he launches accusations against the believer to rob him of his peace and to mar his service. That stream of accusation can bring a sense of condemnation. And what is a greater hindrance to effective prayer than an accusing conscience? "Beloved, if our heart does not condemn us, we have confidence before God; and whatever we ask we receive from Him" (1 John 3:21-22).

When the accuser confronted Martin Luther with list after list of his sins, Luther penitently admitted they were all his sins. But then he turned to the accuser and said, "Now write across them all, *'The blood of Jesus His Son cleanses us from all sin'*" (1 John 1:7). Here is the perfect, and adequate answer to every accusation of Satan.

The only one who has the right to bring a charge

against us is the One against whom we have sinned. What does He say to the penitent sinner? "Neither do I condemn you; go your way; from now on sin no more" (John 8:11). In full enjoyment of divine absolution, Paul wrote, "Who shall bring any charge against God's elect? Who is to condemn?" Certainly not the Christ who died to put away our sins. No longer do we need to succumb to the condemnation of the accuser. We need only to rise up and use the sword of the Spirit as Martin Luther did.

The Prince of This World
The God of This World

Jesus gave Satan the title of prince, or ruler, of this world. *"The prince of this world is coming"* (John 14:30, RSV, italics added). Paul referred to him as the god of this world. "In their case *the god of this world* has blinded the minds of the unbelievers" (2 Corinthians 4:4, RSV, italics added).

A clear implication is that he heads up the present godless world-system. He is the ruler of a world so organized as to exclude God, a world established on the principles of selfishness and greed, expressing itself in atheistic philosophy and unbridled violence. He is recognized as possessing the power of death (Hebrews 2:14), but His ascendancy is not permanent. Jesus announced, "Now judgment is upon this world; now the ruler of this world shall be cast out" (John 12:31).

The Prince of the Domain of the Air

"You formerly walked according to the course of this world, according to *the prince of the power of the air*" (Ephesians 2:2, italics added).

The question naturally arises, What is meant by "the air" in this title? Should we take it literally or figurative-

ly? William Hendriksen discusses the question helpfully in
his book on Ephesians. He writes:

> If, therefore, according to the consistent doctrine of
> Scripture, the evil spirits must be *somewhere,* but not in
> the heaven of the redeemed, and if in this present age
> they cannot be restricted to hell, is it so strange that
> Ephesians 2:2 speaks about "the prince of the domain of
> the air"? Is it not rather natural that the prince of evil is
> able, as far as God in his overruling providence permits,
> to carry on his sinister work by sending his legions to our
> globe and its surrounding atmosphere?
>
> Does not Ephesians 6:12 (the spiritual forces of evil in
> the heavenly places) point in this same general direc-
> tion? . . . This passage, in conjunction with others, clear-
> ly teaches that God has tenanted the supermundane
> realm with innumerable hosts, and that in its lower re-
> gion the minions of Satan are engaged in their destruc-
> tive missions?[2]

We have considered the significance of fourteen of the
thirty names and titles applied to the devil. A clear and
consistent picture emerges.

When J. B. Phillips, the Bible translator, told a televi-
sion audience of the effect his immersion in the gospels
in the course of his translation work had had on him, he
said, "It resulted in the emergence of a Figure so much
greater than man, that I could only gasp incredulously.
In the incarnation, the incredible humility of God struck
me with overwhelming awe."

As we ponder the significance of the devil's names,
what kind of picture emerges?

THE APE OF GOD

It was St. Augustine who called the devil *Simius Dei,*
the ape, the imitator, of God. That concept finds support

in Paul's warning in 2 Corinthians: "For such men are false apostles, deceitful workers, disguising themselves as apostles of Christ. And no wonder, for even *Satan disguises himself as an angel of light*" (11:13-14, italics added).

In Revelation 13:11 John writes, "And I saw another beast coming up out of the earth; and he had two horns like a lamb, and spoke as a dragon." The identity of the beast is clear from the context. The dragon apes the Lamb. Satan imitates God. He sets up his own counterfeit religious system in imitation of Christianity.

Satan has his own *trinity*—the devil, the beast, and the false prophet (Revelation 16:13). He has his own *church,* "a synagogue of Satan" (Revelation 2:9). He has his own *ministers,* "ministers of Satan" (2 Corinthians 11:4-5). He has formulated his own *system of theology,* "doctrines of demons" (1 Timothy 4:1). He has established his own *sacrificial system;* "The Gentiles . . . sacrifice to demons" (1 Corinthians 10:20). He has his own *communion service,* "the cup of demons . . . and the table of demons" (1 Corinthians 10:21). His ministers proclaim *his own gospel,* "a gospel contrary to that which we have preached to you" (Galatians 1:7-8). He has his own *throne* (Revelation 13:2) and his own worshipers (Revelation 13:4).

So he has developed a thorough imitation of Christianity, viewed as a system of religion. In his role as the imitator of God, he inspires *false christs,* self-constituted messiahs (Matthew 24:4-5). He employs *false teachers* who are specialists in his "theology," to bring in "destructive heresies, even denying the Master who bought them" (2 Peter 2:1). They are adept at mixing truth and error in such proportions as to make error palatable. They carry on their teaching surreptitiously and often anonymously.

He sends out *false prophets.* "And many false prophets will arise, and will mislead many" (Matthew 24:11). He introduces *false brethren* into the church, who "had sneaked in to spy out our liberty. . . in order to bring us into bondage" (Galatians 2:4). He sponsors *false apostles* who imitate the true (2 Corinthians 11:13).

It has been well said that "all that which the Lord does well, he (the devil) caricatures badly or in evil."

A STARTLING CONTRAST

The characteristics and nature of the devil are striking when he and his activities are contrasted with the Holy Spirit and His gracious ministries. He is the antithesis of the Holy Spirit in every way. The Holy Spirit, a real person, was sent by the Father and the Son to regenerate and sanctify God's people and to equip them for God's service. Satan, also a real person, is implacably committed to draw men away from God and His salvation, and to thwart the progress of His gospel.

Hear the testimony of Scripture on these contrasts:

The Holy Spirit is the Spirit of truth; the devil is the spirit of error (1 John 4:6).

The Holy Spirit is the Spirit of truth; the devil is the father of lies (John 14:17; 8:44).

The Holy Spirit is the life-giving Spirit; the devil was a murderer from the beginning (1 Corinthians 15:45; John 8:44).

The Holy Spirit is the Spirit of holiness; the devil is the author of evil (Romans 1:4; Matthew 6:13).

The Holy Spirit is likened to a harmless dove; the devil is likened to a subtle serpent (Matthew 3:16; Revelation 12:9).

The Holy Spirit is our helper; the devil is our adversary (Romans 8:26; 1 Peter 5:8).

The Holy Spirit is our advocate; the devil is a slanderer (John 14:16; Job 1:9-11).

The devil is "a strong man armed"; the Holy Spirit is "a stronger than he" (Luke 11:21-22).

The Holy Spirit gives men utterance; the devil makes men dumb (Acts 2:4; Mark 9:17).

4

Eden and the Wilderness

There are two prominent events revealed in the history of Satan, falling within the period of time when he proposed in his heart to become like the Most High and his yet future banishment and execution. The first of these was his meeting with and triumph over the first Adam, when he wrested the scepter of authority from man, by securing man's loyal obedience to his own suggestion and counsel. This earthly scepter Satan held by the full right of conquest, seemingly without challenge from Jehovah, until the first advent of the last Adam. . . . He met the Lord Jesus in the wilderness, offering Him all he had gained from the first Adam, even the kingdoms of this world, if only he might . . . receive the obedient worship and adoration of the last Adam. . . .

However victorious Satan may have been over the first Adam, it is certain that he met a complete and final judgment and sentence in the last Adam.[1]

L. S. Chafer

The Temptation of the First Adam

Before considering the initial temptation as recorded in Genesis 3, an important question needs to be answered: How is this narrative interpreted? Is it mythical or allegorical or historical? Those alternatives have been a theological battleground through the centuries. Within the limits of the space available let us consider those three views.

THE MYTHICAL VIEW

Proponents of the *mythical view* maintain the narrative is a myth—truth conveyed in poetic form, probably derived from the folklore of the times or from surrounding nations. The sacred tree, for example, figures in most religions. This view has some features to commend it, but leaves important questions unanswered:

1. Why did Jesus refer to the Eden story as though it were historical fact? (Matthew 19:3-9; Mark 10:29; John 8:44). If He is in error as to the origin of human sin, can His statements be trusted when He speaks about salvation from sin? His testimony is surely final on the matter if the gospels are trustworthy documents.

2. Was Paul similarly in error when he specifically referred to Adam and Eve as historical personages? "The serpent deceived Eve by his craftiness" (2 Corinthians 11:3). "For it was Adam who was created, and then Eve. And it was not Adam who was deceived, but the woman being quite deceived fell into transgression" (1 Timothy 2:13-14). Paul bases his whole doctrine of sin on the historical character of the Genesis story (Romans 5:12). To label it as myth is to undermine his whole teaching.

3. The characteristics of the Hebrew poetic form are absent in this chapter.

4. If the Scripture record is not historical, how did human sin originate? Is it reasonable to suppose that although God gives a full and clear revelation of salvation from sin, He has left us without any clue to the genesis of the sin from which we are to be saved?

THE ALLEGORICAL VIEW

Advocates of *the parabolic or allegorical view*, who see the allegedly historical characters as symbols of something else, also face problems. The artlessness and simplicity of the record argues against it. It does not possess the distinctive features of a parable. If it is a parable, it has no parallel in Scripture.

As to allegory, has anyone ever mistaken John Bunyan's immortal allegory *Pilgrim's Progress* for literal history? Allegory shines out of every page. Yet millions of intelligent people have interpreted the Genesis passage as being authentic history.

Adherents of the allegorical view have difficulty in interpreting their allegory consistently. What does the garden stand for? And the animals? Of what did the temptation consist? What exactly was the punishment symbolized in 3:16-18? Who was the tempter? This view seems to raise quite as many difficulties as it resolves.

THE HISTORICAL VIEW

The historical or literal view simply maintains that the account should be taken in its natural, obvious, and unstrained sense, and be interpreted consistently with the rest of the chapter as a historical narrative. There are strong reasons for adopting this course:

1. There is no suggestion in the narrative itself that it is allegorical.
2. Christ and other Scripture writers uniformly refer to its details as actual history.
3. The geographical locations are historical.
4. There is no intimation in the narrative that it is not historical.
5. The progenitors of the human race were real human beings, not mythical allegorical or legendary beings.

As such they would live on the earth and eat its produce. Neither they nor the fruit of the earth were legendary.

6. The curse on man, woman, and the ground are painfully literal.

7. Scarcely any part of God's Word is more in accord with the known facts of history and science than this chapter.

This view does not obviate the assumption that the two trees were symbolical of spiritual truths, while still being visible realities. The Tabernacle in the wilderness, for example, was symbolic of spiritual truths, yet was an objective reality.

In view of the above factors, these words of Dr. W. H. Griffith Thomas express the most reasonable and probable explanation of the present condition and plight of man:

> The truest method of interpretation is that which regards these narratives as pictorial records of actual fact; solid history in pictorial form. It is inadequate to speak of the narrative as poetic or merely symbolic, lest we give the impression that the story is not concerned with actual fact. Allegory, too, is identical with the truth illustrated, and does not necessarily presuppose any historical basis. What we must insist on and ever keep in view is that whether allegorical or pictorial, the narrative is expressive of actual fact.[2]

On that basis, let us consider the temptation of the primal pair, an incident of seminal importance. The hermeneutical "law of first mention" in Scripture holds that when a subject is first mentioned, certain important and fundamental concepts are often communicated, which throw light on its subsequent use in Scripture.

The account of the temptation of the first Adam in

Eden, where the serpent, later identified as Satan, is first mentioned, gives important clues to his nature and methods of operation. Although Satan is not specifically mentioned, both Paul and John identify him with the serpent (2 Corinthians 11:3,14). "The serpent of old who is called the devil and Satan" (Revelation 12:9).

One of the Hebrew words for *serpent* can mean "to shine." It would be a reasonable inference in the light of the curse pronounced on it, that the serpent in Eden was not as now, the lowest, most loathed of the animal creation. Rather it was characterized by beauty and splendor. Obviously, there was nothing in it to awaken revulsion in Eve or to create any suspicion of a sinister purpose.

A careful reading of the passage makes it very difficult not to see a subtlety at work above that of a serpent. No irrational creature could have precipitated such world-shaking results with such subtle and consummate skill. It has been suggested that just as the speaking of Balaam's ass was a divine miracle, so the speaking of the serpent was a diabolical miracle.

If it is suggested that there was no objective tempter, and that the conversation was only a conflict in Eve's mind clothed in parabolic form, that by no means dissolves the difficulties. What was the occasion to induce the evil and calamity that so clearly afflicted the human race? And whence the thoughts Eve entertained, since she came perfect from the hand of God? If no serpent was involved, why the pronouncement of such a solemn curse on it? And what does the curse on the serpent *mean?* If there was no serpent, what of the enmity between the two seeds?

From his appropriation of an animal's body for his subtle purpose, the inference is that Satan cannot materialize at will. In the theophanies of the Old Testament, Jehovah appeared in human form. But there is nothing to suggest that Satan possesses that power. It is, however, recorded that "Satan entered into Judas" and used his body as the instrument of his foul design. "Spiritual evil took material form, to reach the spirit of man through the material part of his being."

Paul set the incident in clear light when he wrote, "The serpent deceived Eve by his craftiness" (2 Corinthians 11:3). The first revelation of his character in the Bible is in the role of a deceiver, and he runs true to form through the remainder of the Book. The method of his attack on Eve's faith and integrity should alert us to the subtlety of his approach.

FACTORS IN THE TEMPTATION

Note some of the factors present in Eve's temptation:
1. Satan approached her when she was alone and without the support of her husband. Temptation is essentially a lonely experience.
2. Satan was careful not to appear in a form that would terrorize her or arouse revulsion. That would only throw her back into the arms of God. Instead, he chose as his instrument an attractive but inferior animal.
3. Satan did not shock her by suggesting some blatant blasphemy of God, only the harmless, pleasant gratification of natural desire—but out of the will of God.
4. Satan gave no impression of being the implacable enemy of God. True, his references to God were denigrating, but not blatantly so.

Then note *the elements of the temptation* that led to the fatal fall. John summarized the constituent elements of the world as "the lust of the flesh and the lust of the eyes and the boastful pride of life" (1 John 2:16). Each of those elements is present in this first attack of the god of this world on the first man.

"The woman saw that it was good for food"—the lust of the flesh—"and that it was a delight to the eyes"—the lust of the eyes—"and that the tree was to be desired to make one wise"—the pride of life.

Satan seduced her into rebellion and disobedience by playing on her bodily appetites, her aesthetic sense, and by arousing in her an unholy ambition—"your eyes will be opened, and you will be like God, knowing good and evil."

METHOD OF THE TEMPTATION

The method of the temptation was no less subtle than its substance. First, by apparently innocuous questions and gentle insinuations, Satan aroused Eve's curiosity. Then he subtly cast suspicion on God's love and disinterested goodness, and planted the seeds of doubt of the integrity of God and of His word. Indeed, he distorted God's words to suit his own sinister purpose. Finally, he flatly denied God's word and laughed away the idea of penalty for breaking the divine prohibition.

The steps in Eve's downfall are solemn instruction for us all as we face similar enticements from the evil one. What were those downward steps?

1. Instead of immediately rejecting any aspersion on her Benefactor who had done her only good, she listened to Satan's slander. If we allow thought-room to slanders on God, we have started on the road to capitulation.
2. She began to doubt God's benevolence.
3. That opened the door to questioning the veracity of

His word.

4. She exaggerated the divine prohibition (cf. Genesis 2:16-17 with 3:3).

5. She minimized the penalty God had pronounced (cf. Genesis 2:17 with 3:3).

6. She longed for what God had forbidden.

7. She defied God's prohibition. And not content with that, she enticed her husband to do the same.

Two other facts emerge. One, since Adam and Eve came perfect from the hand of God, with no evil strain, evil must have come from without, from a source other than human. The other fact is that this incident affords us insight into the devil's consistent attitude towards the Word of God. He will quote it or misquote it, as best suits his purpose. He will distort it, deny it, discredit it. But there is one thing he is powerless to do—he cannot affect its absolute truth, for "the Scripture cannot be broken."

Thus, in the very first mention of our great adversary in the Bible, we hear clear warning of his subtlety and of the sinister nature of temptations we, too, must face.

BRUISING THE SERPENT'S HEAD

It is both striking and comforting that, in the very verse in which God pronounced sentence on the serpent, He gave the first intimation, obscure though it appeared, of a gospel of deliverance from the power of Satan: "I will put enmity between you and the woman, and between her seed and your seed; *he shall bruise you on the head,* and you shall bruise him on the heel" (Genesis 3:15, italics added). Only in the light of what has happened in intervening centuries can we see the tremendous implications of that cryptic prophecy.

The expression "the seed of the woman" is both

strange and unique. The seed is always that of the man. Without asserting this is a prediction of the virgin birth, one may say the unusual grammatical construction opens the way for that unique event.

Again, the terms of the sentence and prophecy intimate the seed (singular) of the woman would crush not only the seed of the serpent, but also the serpent himself. "And the God of peace will soon crush Satan under your feet" (Romans 16:20). The picture derives from the ancient custom of the victorious king who placed his feet on the neck of the king he has conquered to symbolize complete subjugation (Joshua 10:24).

> Jesus the prisoner's fetters breaks,
>   And bruises Satan's head,
> Power into strengthless souls He speaks,
>   And life into the dead.
>   Charles Wesley

THE MOST SUITABLE INSTRUMENT

In the Edenic temptation, Satan's subtlety in seducing the believer into sin and rebellion against God is seen not only in his choice of the most favorable occasion, but also in his selection of the most suitable human instrument. This comes at the dawn of human history.

God formed Eve as Adam's wife because "for the man there was not found a helper for him." Adam and Eve became one. They enjoyed not only their own company but also happy fellowship with God. Then tragedy struck. The one whom God gave Adam to be his helper became the instrument of his fall. The tragedy that ultimately engulfed the whole race is stated with great economy of words:

> When the woman saw that the tree was good for food, and that it was a delight to the eyes, and that the tree was

desirable to make one wise, she took from its fruit and ate; she gave also to her husband with her, and he ate. [Genesis 3:6]

Satan achieved his objective of breaking down Adam's loyalty to God by playing upon his natural affection. Eve was deceived by the tempter. But Adam sinned with his eyes open. He placed affection for his wife before love for his God and in so doing involved the whole human race in ruin.

When Job was tested in the crucible of suffering, he held fast to his integrity and his faith in the goodness of God in the face of an avalanche of troubles. But then, with divine permission, Satan "smote Job with sore boils from the sole of his foot to the crown of his head. . . . Then his wife said to him, 'Do you still hold fast your integrity? Curse God and die!' " (Job 2:7-9).

Once again Satan tried the ruse that had seduced Adam into rebellion. He used as his agent of temptation the one who should have given Job the strongest support. But where Adam fell, Job stood firm. Hear his confession of unshaken confidence in God: "But he said to her, 'You speak as one of the foolish women speaks. Shall we indeed accept good from God and not accept adversity?' " (2:10).

Even the loyal but impetuous Peter was the unwitting servant of Satan when he offered a suggestion which, if followed, would have deflected Jesus from His path to the cross:

Peter took him aside and began to rebuke Him, saying, "God forbid it, Lord! This shall never happen to You!" Or as another rendering has it, "Pity yourself Lord!" But He turned and said to Peter, "Get behind Me, Satan! You are a stumbling block to Me; for you are not setting your mind on God's interests, but man's (Matthew 16:23).

THE TEMPTATION OF THE SECOND ADAM

The arrogance and effrontery of Satan know no bounds. He will challenge even the Son of God to a trial of strength. He had scored a resounding victory over the first Adam in the Garden of Eden. Now he would put the second Adam to the test in the barren desert.

A PERSONAL TEMPTER

There was no one with Jesus in the desert and no witness to the temptation. So it is reasonable to conclude that the account of that event given by the evangelists came directly from His lips. The language used leaves the clear impression that He met a personal tempter in fierce conflict (see Matthew 4:3-11):

> "The tempter came and said to him"
> "The devil took him to the holy city"
> "He answered, It is written"
> "Jesus said to him"
> "Then the devil left him"

It is quite impossible to make the language fit the concept of an impersonal force or influence, or a personification of evil. It was a confrontation of personalities. Nor is it admissible to suggest that Jesus was engaged in an inner conflict with His own desires and ambitions. If He did not confront a factual, personal devil, as the Scripture account records, the only alternative is to suggest that His temptations came from within His own personality. That would presuppose a disposition to evil within Him, a possibility that Scripture specifically excludes. "In Him was no sin," essentially. "He *knew no sin,*" experientially. "He *did* no sin," factually.

Note that, in reality, the temptation was not initiated by the devil. The conflict was neither incidental nor accidental. It was an open challenge to the usurper, specifically induced by God. "Then Jesus was led up by the Spirit into the wilderness to be tempted by the devil" (Matthew 4:1). The reason the Son of God appeared, wrote John, was to "destroy the works of the devil" (1 John 3:8). This was the first major engagement in the protracted conflict.

THE EDEN TEMPTATION REPEATED

The elements and methods adopted by Satan in his conquest of the first Adam reappear in the desert. His subtlety shows in the apparent naturalness and reasonableness of his suggestions. After a long fast, what was more right and natural than to satisfy one's hunger? What more appropriate way was there to establish Jesus' divine Sonship than for Him to perform a dramatic miracle? If there were an easier way to the throne promised Him than the pathway of suffering and rejection, why not take it?

But in each temptation was a skillfully concealed hook. For Jesus to have yielded would have involved His acting independently of and contrary to His Father. True, He could have satisfied a legitimate appetite, but by adopting illegitimate means. He could have produced a type of spiritual result, but by means contrary to His Father's will. He could have gained a heritage, but not the one His Father had prepared for Him.

AVENUES OF TEMPTATION

A study of the three temptations reveals them as representative temptations that covered the whole range of human desire.

The writer of Hebrews tell us that we have "a high priest who . . . has been tempted in all things as we are,

yet without sin" (4:15). Does that mean that Jesus suffered every specific temptation that man has suffered
through the ages? Manifestly not. For example, how
could He have suffered the temptations peculiar to the
space age? Does it not mean, rather, that temptation as-
sailed Him in its full force *along every avenue in which
it can reach our human nature?* Surrounding circumstances and incidental details may differ widely. But, in
essence, temptations are the same for all men in all ages.

Essentially, temptation assails man along only three
lines. All other temptations are only variants of these. It
is not surpising, then, to find that these three elements
are present in both the temptation in Eden and the temptation in the desert.

The first avenue is *appetite, the desire to enjoy things*
(Matthew 4:2-4). John calls this "the lust of the flesh"
(1 John 2:16).

Since Jesus was hungry, Satan made his first approach
on the physical plane in the realm of legitimate appetite. The devil appeared in the role of a benefactor. Why
should Jesus not appease His hunger by using His inherent power to turn stones into bread? Is not desire for
food an innocent, God-given instinct? Since He was Son
of God, why not exercise His undoubted powers to gratify a perfectly legitimate desire?

The temptation was so insidious, so plausible, that
few of us would have detected in it the cloven hoof. But
the focus of the temptation was not on His right to
gratify His hunger, but on *His submission to the will of
God.* In each temptation the devil tried to induce Jesus
to act in a manner contrary to complete dependence on
God, by acting independently and in self-interest.

His method of quenching and deflecting the adversary's fiery dart was simple but effective. The same Spirit

who led Him into conflict recalled to His mind a relevant passage of Scripture that laid bare the true nature
of the temptation. "It is written, MAN SHALL NOT LIVE ON
BREAD ALONE, BUT ON EVERY WORD THAT PROCEEDS OUT OF THE
MOUTH OF GOD" (Matthew 4:4). On His lips, those words
expressed His complete confidence that His Father
would supply Him with needed bread in His own way
and time.

He refused to employ His divine prerogatives to gratify His natural desires. To yield to the satanic suggestion
would be tantamount to denial of His incarnation. He
would be "calling into His service powers which His
brethren could not employ"—and defeat the very purpose of His advent.

Further, it would have been satisfying a legitimate
craving in an illegitimate manner. He preferred remain-
ing ravenously hungry to moving out of line with His
Father's will. Had He yielded to the tempter's wiles and
used His powers to provide bread by a miracle, His call
to discipleship would have lost much of its appeal for
those who possessed no such powers.

The second avenue along which temptation can assail
man is *ambition, the desire the achieve things* (Matthew 4:5-6). This John designates as "the pride of life"
(1 John 2:16).

The scene now changes. Satan takes Jesus from the
arid desert to the top of the Temple. The pinnacle—or
better, parapet—was in all probability the southern
wing, which overlooked the Kidron Valley hundreds of
feet below. Josephus asserted that "anyone looking down
would be giddy, while his sight would not reach to such
an immense depth." It appears that Satan's suggestion
was for Jesus to leap not into the crowded Temple court,
but into the abyss.

The focus of this second temptation was on *our Lord's confidence in God.* The tempter buttressed His proposition with an apt quotation from Scripture. But in doing so, with consummate subtlety, he omitted the vital phrase "in all your ways" (cf. Luke 4:10-11 with Psalm 91:11-12). He challenged Jesus to demonstrate His faith in the Father by putting His promise to the test.

The Master replied that for Him to do this would not be *faith,* but *presumption.* He refused to go beyond the limits God had laid down for Him, and thus tempt God. God is not bound to respond to "every irresponsible whim of the want of faith." Stunting was not one of God's ways, nor was it one of Jesus'. The Jews looked for a Messiah who would work dazzling wonders and thus establish a worldwide empire with Jerusalem as its center. To succumb to the devil's temptation would be to yield to their carnal expectations.

Note Christ's repeated use of the formula "It is written." He knew how to wield "the sword of the Spirit which is the word of God." He saw to the heart of the temptation and applied appropriate scriptural and spiritual principles to the situation. Each Scripture He used revealed *God's view* of the factors involved in the temptation. In this case He would not presumptuously court danger, for that was clearly not the will of His Father. He refused to establish His rightful kingdom by outward show.

Foiled again, the tempter made a last bid to seduce Jesus from the path of faith and of obedience to His Father.

The third avenue through which temptation can reach man is *avarice, the desire to get things* (Matthew 4:8-11). John describes it as "the lust of the eyes" (1 John 2:16).

Satan's first assault on our Lord was on the physical plane, the second on the mental. In the third, he invaded the realm of the spiritual. He demanded that Jesus accord to him (Satan) the place that belongs to God alone.

This time he took Jesus to a high mountain. Apparently in a vision—for "all the kingdoms of the world and their glory" could not be seen physically in "a moment of time" from any mountain in Palestine—he presented the glory of world dominion to the Son of Man. The devil offered Him an outward kingdom with its outward pomp and splendor. It is noteworthy that Jesus did not challenge Satan's boast: "I will give You all this domain and its glory; for *it has been handed over to me, and I give it to whomever I wish*" (Luke 4:6, italics added). He did not charge Satan with falsehood, as He would have done had the claim not been true. Further, if it had not been true, it would not have constituted a real temptation.

Jesus had indeed come to win a world-kingdom of power and glory. But it would be according to His Father's way, and He knew that way included an agonizing cross. He perceived that what the devil offered Him was a crown without a cross. The nub of his last assault was the possibility of *evading the anguish and agony of the cross* by a compromise with Satan.

For the second time, our Lord unsheathed the sword of the Spirit and wielded it expertly. "It is written, YOU SHALL WORSHIP THE LORD YOUR GOD, AND SERVE HIM ONLY."

Having failed to storm the citadel of Christ's loyalty and obedience to His Father, the devil left Him, but only until "an opportune time." Later he returned to attack with even greater fury.

For us baptized, for us He bore
His holy fast and hungered sore,
For us temptations sharp He knew,
For us the tempter overthrew.

                          Isaac Watts

It is not without significance that each of the answers
of Jesus to the devil was a quotation from Deuteronomy,
the book against which the strongest assults of destructive criticism have been leveled. It is reassuring that the
Son of God entertained no doubts as to its authenticity
or authority.

And what of the outcome of the temptation?

In relation to the Lord Himself, it issued in unquali-
fied triumph. The subtle suggestions of the evil one left
Him entirely untainted by sin. Nor was His filial relationship with His Father in any way disturbed. He entered on
the ordeal "full of the Spirit." He returned from it "in the
power of the Spirit," enriched and not impoverished.

In relation to the believer, Christ's victory gives assurance of the possibility of our personal triumph over
Satan and his wiles. It holds out the alluring possibility
for us to emerge unscathed from the fiercest temptation.

In relation to Satan himself, the temptation resulted
in ignominious, utter defeat. Each of Jesus' replies dealt
another stunning blow. Satan's subtlety and sophistries
were ruthlessly exposed. His defeat in the desert was the
first step towards his final and absolute defeat at the
consummation of the age.

Cold mountains and the midnight air
Witnessed the fervour of Thy prayer;
The desert Thy temptations knew,
Thy conflict, and Thy victory too.

                          Isaac Watts

5

Rival Hierarchies

*There are two opposing hierarchies, eternally at war.
Good angels in alliance with God, and all saints, to
promote all that is good; evil demons confederate
with each other and all evil men, to work disaster and
ruin, and if it were possible, supplant even the Almighty.*[1]

A. T. Pierson

KING OF HELL?

IT IS A POPULAR BELIEF that as God is King of heaven, so Satan
is king of hell. And that as heaven is the center of God's
administration, so Satan directs his nefarious operations
from hell. But such a conception has no basis in Scripture. Satan never aspired to be king of hell, but king of
heaven. That is perfectly clear from the words expressed
in his vaunting ambition. "I will ascend to heaven; . . . I
will ascend above the heights of the clouds; I will make
myself like the Most High" (Isaiah 14:13-14).

> A safe stronghold our God is still,
>   A trusty shield and weapon;
> He'll help us clear from all the ill
>   That hath us now o'ertaken.
>   The ancient *prince of hell*
>   Hath risen with purpose fell,
>   Strong mail and craft of power

He weareth in this horn
On earth is not his equal.
Martin Luther
(Trans. Thomas Carlyle)

As has been said earlier, popular thought about the devil and his followers has taken its color largely from medieval writings, especially those of Dante and Milton. The latter popularized the idea of Satan's reigning in hell, by naming that as his ambition. But that is the very opposite of the truth. Here are the words Milton put into Satan's mouth:

The mind is its own place, and in itself
Can make a Heaven of Hell, a Hell of Heaven.
What matter where, if I be still the same,
And what I should be, all but less than He
Whom Thunder has made greater? Here at least
We shall be free; the Almighty hath not built
Here for His envy, will not drive us hence;
Here we may reign secure, and *in my choice*
To reign is worth ambition, though in Hell.
Better to reign in Hell than serve in Heaven.

Paradise Lost

There is nothing in the Revelation or in any other part of Scripture to support such a view. Nowhere does it state that Satan is in hell in this present age. He is "the god of this age" and "the prince of the power of the air"—this is his domain and the sphere of his operations in this age. Not until its consummation will he be cast into hell.

And I saw an angel coming down from heaven, having the key of the abyss and a great chain in his hand. And he laid hold of the dragon, the serpent of old, who is the devil and Satan, and bound him for a thousand years, and threw him into the abyss. . . . And when the thousand years are completed. . . . the devil who deceived them was thrown into the lake of fire and brimstone, where the beast and the false prophet are also; and they will be tormented day and night forever and ever. [Revelation 20:1-3,7,10]

So there are no scriptural grounds for supposing that Satan rules as king of hell. He now has a temporary reign, but only as pretender and usurper—and not in hell. When at last he comes to hell, it will be as prisoner, not as king. Meanwhile, he does have a kingdom over which he exercises authority.

Two Hierarchies

Since the time Satan conspired to oust God from the throne of the universe, he himself has been ousted from his place of privilege and has set up a rival kingdom. The existence of those rival kingdoms is clearly recognized in Scripture.

And Satan also is divided against himself, how shall *his kingdom* stand? [Luke 11:18, italics added]

And they will come from east and west, and from north and south, and will recline at the table in *the kingdom of God*. [Luke 13:29, italics added]

Unless one is born of water and the Spirit, he cannot enter into *the kingdom of God*. [John 3:5, italics added]

The subjects of the kingdom of God are those who acknowledge the Saviorhood and Lordship of Christ and have accepted His sovereignty. The subjects of the kingdom of Satan are those who do not acknowledge Christ's Saviorhood and Lordship. They do not acknowledge His Kingship. Note that Satan is called "the ruler of this world" (John 12:31), but never "the king of this world." He maintains his claims only as a traitor and a usurper. His followers acknowledge him, whether consciously or unconsciously, as "the god of this world" (2 Corinthians 4:4).

These two kingdoms are further contrasted as the *kingdom of darkness* and the *kingdom of light.* "For He delivered us from the domain of darkness, and transferred us to the kingdom of His beloved Son" (Colossians 1:13). Sin is characterized by darkness and death, righteousness by light and life.

In commissioning Paul as the apostle to the Gentiles, the risen Lord said, "But arise . . . for this purpose I have appeared to you . . . to open their eyes so that they may turn *from darkness to light* and *from the dominion of Satan to God*" (Acts 26:16,18, italics added). Paul identifies that sphere of darkness as the domain of Satan's authority in which men are caught and held.

THE HIERARCHY OF SATAN

God's kingdom is so organized that His will is executed through angels to whom He has delegated authority to rule and serve under Him. Each rank of angels has his assigned sphere and special responsibilities. Paul refers to gradations in these spirit beings: "thrones, dominions, rulers, authorities" (Colossians 1:16).

In imitating the kingdom of God, Satan organized his kingdom of darkness along similar lines. He works through gradations of the demons implicated with him in his fall. It appears some of those evil spirits have regional authority, for example, "prince of Persia" and "the prince of Greece" (Daniel 10:-13,20).

Paul refers to evil spirits as "rulers," "powers," "world forces of this darkness," and "spiritual forces of wickedness in the heavenly places" (Ephesians 6:12). Those terms were in common use in the angelology of Paul's day. It is likely he used current terms to assert the supremacy of Christ over all possible existences, whether celestial or terrestrial. We may not be able to assign any exact significance to each of those terms, but some possibilities seem appropriate:

Rulers may be princes in Satan's kingdom who have been assigned authority over specific regions and who work in the political realm.

Powers may signify evil spirits of energy and force who, at Satan's instigation, incite men to acts of violence.

World forces of this darkness may indicate the evil spirits that foster sorcery, astrology, superstition, spiritism, idolatry, and so on, whose aim it is to keep men in spiritual darkness.

Spiritual forces of wickedness in the heavenlies may be those spirits who invade the realm of religious experience in the guise of angels of light and lure men from truth and holiness into corruption and wickedness.

Scripture presents a consistent picture of these two rival hierarchies as they wage truceless warfare. Since both God and Satan concentrate on men in an endeavor to win their loyalty and cooperation, the Christian finds himself at the center of a cunningly waged war. God and all the good angels are concerned with the highest good for man. Satan and his evil demons are allied with evil men to effect man's ruin. Between the two hierarchies is war to the death.

Satan knows his ultimate defeat is certain. And as he sees the rapidly approaching date of the execution of sentence already pronounced on him (Revelation 12:12), in great wrath he does all in his power to postpone that event as long as possible.

The World, or the Satanic System

It is appropriate to consider the nature of the world that constitutes his kingdom. What a web is to a spider, what bait is to the angler, what a lure is to the fowler, so is the world to Satan a means of capturing men.

What is the world of which Satan is god? To differentiate this word—*kosmos*—from other words translated "world," it might be helpful to adopt the term "world-system," for that is its connotation. The world, as Paul and John used it, is human society organized in such a way as to exclude God, to make Him superfluous. It refers to the great evil system over which Satan exercises despotic power. Its master principles are not love and self-sacrifice, but selfishness, greed, ambition, pleasure, and force (Matthew 4:8-9; John 12:31; 18:36; Ephesians 2:2; 1 John 2:15-17).

"We know," wrote John, ". . . the whole world lies in the power of the evil one" (1 John 5:19). As its presiding genius, Satan enunciates its objectives and plots its policies. The world embraces all unregenerated men whether amiable or unlovable, because they are united in a common desire and purpose to be independent of God. It is called "this evil world," and it hates the Christ who testified of it "that its deeds are evil" (John 7:7).

Concerning the satanic world-system, C. I. Scofield writes:

> It is imposing and powerful with armies and fleets; is often outwardly religious, scientific, cultured and elegant; but seething with national and commercial rivalries and ambitions; is upheld in any real crisis only by armed force, and is dominated by Satanic principles.[2]

It was the kingdoms of this world that the devil offered Jesus in the wilderness. The expression "the kingdoms of the world" used by Satan in the temptation was in common use to describe the Roman Empire, which grasped most of the known world in its tentacles. The control of the world was surrendered to Satan by the first man, who yielded his God-given sovereignty over the earth and creation to the usurper. Even after Calvary's victory, when Christ won back man's forfeited inheritance, Satan's control of this world-system has been permitted to continue for reasons that God deems wise.

It is not difficult to recognize the hallmark of satanic control of the world-system in the corruption, deceit, and pollution that characterizes its policies and politics.

6

Demons and Demon Possession

Man is especially open to all influences of the spirit realm, whether good or bad. Just as his bodily organism makes him accessible to impressions from physical nature, and his animal life and intelligence to contact with all forms of conscious life, so his spiritual being responds to the unseen approach of other spirits, who are as distinctly personal as himself, but not limited to sense channels for contact. [1]

A. T. Pierson

A COMPARISON of the New Testament teachings on demonology with Babylonian ideas and even Jewish rabbinical sources, reveals the incomparable superiority of divine revelation. L. M. Sweet affirms that in the former there are none of the grotesque fancies that abound in the latter.

Of the eighty references to demons in the New Testament, in eleven instances the distinction between demon possession and other diseases is clearly made. Take Matthew 4:24: "They brought to Him all who were ill, taken with various diseases and pains, demoniacs, epileptics, paralytics; and He healed them." The results of demon possession appear to be purely mental in only two cases (Matthew 8:28 and Acts 19:13). Epilepsy is specified in two cases (Matthew 17:15).

There is a distinction made between diseases caused by demons and the same diseases not so caused: "Then there was brought to Him a demon-possessed man who was blind and dumb, and He healed him, so that the dumb man spoke and saw" (Matthew 12:22). "And great multitudes came to Him, bringing with them those who were lame, crippled, blind, dumb, and many others . . . and He healed them" (Matthew 15:30).

Those who have lived in heathen lands and have witnessed the unspeakable cruelties a fear of evil spirits inspires have no illusion as to the accuracy and significance of the biblical records.

THE EXISTENCE OF DEMONS

If we accept the reality of the devil's existence on the authority of Christ, then we have the same reasons for believing in the existence of the demons, of whom he is said to be the prince.

They are called *evil spirits* six times and *unclean spirits* twenty-three times in the New Testament. Those terms are interchangeable with *demons,* for both are used of the one person. "A certain man from the city who was possessed with demons. . . . He had been commanding the unclean spirit to come out of the man." (Luke 8:27,29). These are not the spirits of dead people, as some Jewish authorities believed and as many pagans still believe, but are referred to as the devil's *angels.* Jesus referred to "the eternal fire which has been prepared for the devil and his angels" (Matthew 25:41). They are termed the "angels who did not keep their own domain, but abandoned their proper abode" (Jude 6).

From various Scriptures, it appears that before creating man, God created myriads of angels of varying ranks. Lucifer was the head. When his mysterious revolt took place, he drew with him in his fall multitudes of those angels. They are in league with him in his conflict against God and His holy angels. "And there was war in heaven, Michael and his angels waging war with the dragon. And the dragon and his angels waged war and they were not strong enough" (Revelation 12:7-8).

Some of those evil spirits, fallen angels, are at large, seeking rest. "Now when the unclean spirit goes out of a man, it passes through waterless places, seeking rest, and does not find it" (Matthew 12:43). They are of great number. "For He had been saying to him, 'Come out of the man, you unclean spirit!' And He was asking him, 'What is your name?' And he said to him, 'My name is Legion; for we are many' " (Mark 5:8-9). Because of their great numbers, the emissaries of Satan give him a kind of limited omnipresence.

Other demons are imprisoned in Tartarus, whether for more hellish wickedness or for some other reason is not revealed. "For if God did not spare angels when they sinned, but cast them into hell and committed them to pits of darkness, reserved for judgment" (2 Peter 2:4). "And angels who did not keep their own domain . . . He has kept in eternal bonds under darkness for the judgment of the great day" (Jude 6).

THE NATURE OF DEMONS

1. They are *spiritual* beings, and as such are not material. Jesus said, "Touch Me and see, for a spirit does not have flesh and bones as you see that I have" (Luke 24:39). Being spirits they are independent of matter.
2. They are *personal* beings. Personality and corporeality are not to be confused. God is spirit, but He is not corporeal. The same arguments used to prove

the personality of God can also be used to demonstrate the personality of demons. They have the power of thought, speech, and of action (Acts 19:15-16), since they have power to influence a human personality. The fact they "did not keep their own domain but abandoned their proper abode" (Jude 6) and that they sinned (2 Peter 2:4), shows they had the power of moral choice. They were sensitive to fear (Luke 8:31), and had the power of rage (Matthew 8:28).

3. They are *intelligent* beings. The unclean spirit who controlled the man in the synagogue cried out, "I know who You are—the Holy One of God" (Mark 1:24). Their replies to Christ were couched in intelligent language. The evil spirit said to the sons of Sceva, "Jesus I know, and Paul I know, but who are you?" He could discern the true from the false. Some have suggested that the Greek word *demon* derives from a word meaning "intelligent." But their intelligence is debased and devoted to evil purposes.

4. They are *invisible* beings. Being incorporeal, they are neither visible nor tangible. There is no record in Scripture of their taking visible or tangible form.

5. They are *believing* beings. There are no atheists among them. "You believe that God is one. You do well; the demons also believe, and shudder" (James 2:19). They have faith, but not saving faith, for it does not lead them to repentance. They recognize and confess the deity of Christ, but refuse to give Him their allegiance. They also know who are true believers, and they obey the authority of Jesus' name (Acts 19:15).

6. They are *incorporeal* beings, but seem to have a

strange passion to possess living organisms, whether human or animal. "The demons entreated Him, saying, 'Send us into the swine so that we may enter them.' . . . The unclean spirits entered the swine" (Mark 5:12-13). "Then it goes, and takes along with it seven other spirits more wicked than itself, and they go in and live there; and the last state of that man becomes worse than the first" (Matthew 12:45). It appears they must have control of bodily organs to enable them to execute their hellish assignments. Having once gained control over a human body, they seem to be able to come and go at will. "When the unclean spirit goes out of a man, it passes through waterless places seeking rest, and not finding any, it says, 'I will return to my house from which I came' " (Luke 11:24).

7. They are *powerful* beings, and exercise superhuman strength. And they are also able to impart superhuman strength to their victims. "A certain man . . . who was possessed with demons; . . . He was bound with chains and shackles . . . yet he would burst his fetters" (Luke 8:27,29). They delight to make use of human bodies for evil purposes.

8. They are *innumerable* and well organized, so they can represent their prince in any part of the world (Mark 5:9; Luke 8:30; Matthew 12:28-27).

9. Their first estate, like that of Adam and Eve, was *probationary.* Endowed with free will, they could renounce their allegiance to God. When Satan (their leader) fell, they allied themselves with him in rebellion. Those who shared his rebellion were condemned with him and were not granted any further probation. "For . . . God did not spare angels when they sinned" (2 Peter 2:4). It is probable the

demons who serve Satan now were his agents when he was "the anointed cherub."

10. They are painfully *aware of their impending doom.* "What do we have to do with You, Son of God? Have you come here to torment us *before the time?"* (Matthew 8:29, italics added).

11. They are all wicked, but *not all equally wicked.* The unclean spirit who had gone out of a man returned with "seven other spirits *more wicked than itself"* (Matthew 12:45, italics added).

12. *Their destiny* is "the eternal fire which has been prepared for the devil and his angels" (Matthew 25:41).

13. They have power to *inflict physical disabilities.* "My son, possessed with a spirit which makes him mute; and whenever it seizes him, it dashes him to the ground and he foams at the mouth, and grinds his teeth" (Mark 9:17-18).

DEMON POSSESSION

"There is no reason," writes Dr. L. L. Morris, "why we should reject *a priori* the whole concept of demon possession. When the gospels give us good evidence that it did take place, it is best to accept this."[2]

Scripture teaching is clear that evil spirits have access to man's spiritual being and can influence him for good or evil. It is part of the human situation that man can be influenced, now by a good and now by an evil spirit. Of many references to demon-possessed people we select these:

> And He was casting out a demon, and it was dumb; and it came about that when the demon had gone out, the dumb man spoke; and the multitudes marveled. [Luke 11:14]

> And the news about Him went out into all Syria; and

they brought to Him all who were ill, taken with various diseases and pains, demoniacs, epileptics, paralytics; and He healed them. [Matthew 4:24]

Teacher, I brought You my son, possessed with a spirit which makes him mute; and whenever it seizes him, it dashes him to the ground and he foams at the mouth, and grinds his teeth, and stiffens out. [Mark 9:17-18]

A certain man from the city [met Him] who was possessed with demons; and who had not put on any clothing for a long time, and was not living in a house, but in the tombs. . . . He was bound with chains and shackles . . . yet he would burst his fetters and be driven by the demon into the desert. [Luke 8:27-29]

Many today hold the view that demon possession was only the way people of that day referred to what we would term mental sickness or epilepsy. But a careful examination of Scripture terminology reveals that these two things are clearly differentiated. Note in Matthew 4:24 the variety of terms used, none identical. Demoniacs are specifically distinguished from epileptics.

In New Testament times, when people suffered from an especially severe form of disease, their contemporaries said they had a demon. The seemingly ascetic habits of John the Baptist and the unusual teachings of Jesus drew the same accusation. "John came neither eating nor drinking, and they say, 'He has a demon' " (Matthew 11:18). Jesus said, "If anyone keeps My word he shall never see death." The Jews said to Him, "Now we know that You have a demon" (John 8:51-52). But that popular and often unwarranted belief should not blind us to the realities of actual demon possession.

The gospels evince that the incarnation of God in

Christ unleashed unprecedented demonic fury and activity. The presence on earth of Satan's archrival could not go unchallenged. The purity and power of His holy life could only attract the attentions of the unholy one. The light of truth always arouses the powers of darkness.

Jesus differentiated between ordinary illnesses and demon-induced illnesses. He healed the former by laying on His hands, anointing the eyes, commanding them to go and wash. He healed the latter by exorcising the demon responsible for the disorder. Note the differentiation in this verse: "And He said to them, 'Go and tell that fox [Herod], Behold, *I cast out demons and perform cures* today and tomorrow'" (Luke 13:32, italics added). And again: *"Heal the sick,* raise the dead, cleanse the lepers, *cast out demons"* (Matthew 10:8, italics added). "And they were casting out many demons and were anointing with oil many sick people and healing them" (Mark 6:13).

When Jesus exorcised the demon who had caused blindness and dumbness to one man, the Pharisees attributed Christ's power to the devil. "When the Pharisees heard it, they said, 'This man casts out demons only by Beelzebul the ruler of the demons'" (Matthew 12:24).

The *New Bible Dictionary* affirms that most psychologists dismiss the idea of demon possession. They maintain the equivalents of demon possession today as "a particular extensive complex of compulsive phenomena." But there can be an intermediate position. It is possible to hold that a demon can seize on a repressed facet of personality and from that center influence a person's actions. This may produce hysterical blindness or dumbness, or epilepsy. The Bible does not link epilepsy with demon possession. The fits of the boy in Matthew 17:15 seem to indicate more than epilepsy.

There is an instructive incident recorded in Acts 19:13-16. Some Jewish exorcists—sons of a Jewish high priest named Sceva—had witnessed the miraculous cures and exorcisms of Paul and had coveted his power. Noticing that Paul used what they thought was a potent religious formula, "in the name of Jesus," they used it themselves. But to their dismay, the formula failed to work. Instead of overcoming the evil spirit, they themselves were overcome. The name of Jesus on unsanctified lips conveyed no power. The demon did not recognize divine authority from merely human lips. Only those who are authorized by Christ may use His name. "Behold I have given you [my disciples] authority. . . over all the power of the enemy" (Luke 10:19). When we use Christ's name, we act as His representatives.

The demon recognized the counterfeit. Speaking through its victims, he uttered these scathing words:

> I recognize Jesus, and I know about Paul, but who are you? And the man, in whom was the evil spirit, leaped on them and subdued all of them and overpowered them, so that they fled out of that house naked and wounded. [Acts 19:15-16]

It is dangerous for one who is not "in Christ" to intrude into this realm. But Paul's name was feared.

There is both comparison and contrast in Satan's working in those who are "sons of the evil one" (Matthew 13:38) and the working of the Holy Spirit in the "children of God." Satan controls and empowers those who own allegiance to him. "You formerly walked according to the course of this world, according to the prince of the power of the air, of the spirit that is now working in the sons of disobedience" (Ephesians 2:1-2). Contrast that with, "God . . . is at work in you, both to will and to work for His good pleasure" (Philippians 2:13). Just as God by the Holy Spirit empowers His messengers, so the devil imparts his satanic subtlety and strength to his emissaries.

MOTIVATION

What is the motivation of this host of demons? What inspires them to their hellish and destructive ministry?

Positively, it is *loyalty* to their chosen prince, whose kingdom and authority they aim to establish and extend. If all Christ's followers worked as zealously for their King as the demons do for Satan, there would not be two billion unevangelized people in the world! To achieve their objective, they carry out truceless warfare in the interests of their master.

> For our struggle is not against flesh and blood, but against the rulers, against the powers, against the world forces of this darkness, against the spiritual forces of wickedness in the heavenly places. [Ephesians 6:12]

Negatively, their motivation springs from an implacable hatred of Christ. Their inflexible purpose is to destroy His church and disrupt His purposes. They know Christ and are cognizant of His purposes for blessing mankind. Not without a desperate struggle will the massed powers of darkness yield control of a world that lies asleep in the arms of the evil one.

7

Stratagems and Wiles

Putting the two words devices *and* wiles *into one common meaning, we find that Scripture tells us that the workings of Satan's mind, in fraud, trick, stratagem and artifice need not be unknown to us. The reason Paul was able to say that we are not ignorant of these things is, of course, because we have the clear revelation of the teaching of the Word of God concerning them. Surely one of Satan's greatest stratagems has been the attempt to keep men in ignorance of the real nature of his being, and the fraudulent dimensions of his pretensions.* [1]

D. G. Barnhouse

VICTOR HUGO SAID, "A good general must penetrate the brain of his enemy." In more recent times, Field Marshal Lord Montgomery told in his memoirs that when he was assigned to lead the North African campaign of the Allies against the Germans in World War II, his main subject of study was not the terrain on which they would fight, but the character, background, and outlook of his opposite, General Rommel. If he could foresee what strategy Rommel was likely to adopt, then he could take steps to forestall and eventually conquer him. Should we be less prudent in the spiritual warfare in which we are engaged?

On one occasion I was speaking on this subject in Hong Kong. In going over the message with a young Chinese interpreter, he passed on to me a relevant proverb, in which Chinese literature is so rich. "If you know yourself and your adversary clearly, then in a hundred battles you will win a hundred times." But many of us are spiritual illiterates when it comes to a knowledge of our great adversary. Consequently we lose our battles. Let us no longer remain illiterate in this area, but learn the devil's strategy:

STRATEGY WITH UNBELIEVERS

As head of the kingdom of darkness, the devil adopts the strategy of blinding the minds of the unregenerate.

> In whose case the god of this world has blinded the minds of the unbelieving, that they might not see the light of the gospel of the glory of Christ, who is the image of God. [2 Corinthians 4:4]

He dreads the light of God shining into their hearts and revealing to them their state before God. He knows that would cast them back on Him. So long as liberating truth does not penetrate their minds, he will be able to hold them captive. His plan is to keep them unconscious of the seriousness of their condition. "The whole world lies in the power of the evil one" (1 John 5:19). To keep them lulled to sleep and in spiritual darkness, he feeds them wrong thoughts about God, fills their minds with prejudice, ensnares them in false philosophy, or simply occupies their minds with earthly things.

When Paul said, "We are not ignorant of his devices," his meaning was, "We know how his mind works." A *device*, as the word is used here, means "something devised or contrived for bringing about some end or result; a plan or scheme; an ingenious or clever expedient; a plot, stratagem or trick."

What, then, are some of the tricks Satan uses to capture and retain control of the unbeliever?

He snatches away the good seed of the Word. "When anyone hears the word of the kingdom, and *does not understand it,* the evil one comes and snatches away what has been sown in his heart" (Matthew 13:19, italics added). The picture, of course, is of birds swooping down and picking up the grain fallen from the sower's hand on the hard-beaten path. Even so the devil snatches away the good seed of the Word before it can sink into the understanding and be received by faith. That is the activity of the devil whenever the Word is preached. It underlines the fact we should pray *after* preaching as well as *before,* for this subtle stratagem is all too often successful. How frequently the solemn impression of a powerful sermon is dissipated by idle chatter after a service. The good seed is snatched away.

He lulls the unbeliever into a false sense of peace. "When a strong man, fully armed, guards his own homestead, his possessions are undisturbed" (Luke 11:21). The context makes clear that Satan is the strong man who drugs the senses of his victims, assures them there is nothing in God to fear, and no judgment to anticipate. He deflects the shafts of conviction that the Holy Spirit directs at their hearts, and says, "Peace, peace," when there is no peace.

He lays snares for the unwary. "If perhaps God may grant them repentance leading to the knowledge of the truth, and they may come to their senses and escape from the snare of the devil, having been held captive by him to do his will" (2 Timothy 2:25-26). The devil is a master of subtlety, and adept at concealing his snares. He is too wise a hunter to lay snares in the sight of his victims.

He gains advantage over men by concealing his true and sinister purpose, *by masquerading as an angel of light.* "For such men are false apostles, deceitful workers, disguising themselves as apostles of Christ. And no wonder, for even Satan disguises himself as an angel of light" (2 Corinthians 11:13-14). He is much more likely to succeed when he tempts certain people by appearing in the guise of a benefactor than as a foul fiend or a roaring lion.

He deceives those whose minds are not subject to the Word of truth. "The serpent of old who is called the devil and Satan, who deceives the whole world" (Revelation 12:9). He was successful in deceiving Eve. "The woman being quite deceived, fell into transgression" (1 Timothy 2:14), because she entertained doubts the devil injected into her mind concerning the truth of God's word, instead of immediately rejecting the disloyal suggestion. He is still active unceasingly in deceiving men about the integrity and authority of the God's Word. This is the focal point of the great theological controversies of our day.

He mixes truth with error. "While men were sleeping, his enemy came and sowed tares among the wheat. . . . And he [the landowner] said to them, 'An enemy has done this!' " (Matthew 13:25,28). His strategy is to include enough truth in his teaching to make error appear both credible and palatable—the great appeal and hidden danger of many cults in vogue today. So much seems good and true that injection of error is not obvious. To achieve his end, Satan will quote or misquote Scripture as best suits his purpose. He is ingenious. He employs orthodox language, while giving the old words used a new and heterodox content. That is especially true in theological circles, where theological double talk confuses the issues and conceals the error.

THE CULTS AND THE DEVIL

In his inimitable *Screwtape Letters,* C. S. Lewis writes:

There are two equal and opposite errors into which our race can fall about the devils. One is to disbelieve in their existence. The other is to believe and feel an excessive and unhealthy interest in them.[2]

It is into the first error that many of the modern cults have been seduced by our cunning adversary. Without a shadow of biblical support, the existence of the devil is flatly denied. Here are the assertions of some cults, which should put us on guard.

Theosophy: There is no personal devil. That which is mystically called the devil is the negation and opposite of God. The devil is not to be confounded with Satan, though they are sometimes spoken of in Scripture as if they were identical. In such cases Scripture presents the popular belief.

Unity School of Christianity: There is no personal devil.

Spiritism: There is no devil and no evil spirits. All spirit-people of wisdom know that there is no fearful devil. All spirits in the other world are nothing else but the souls of those who have lived here.

Christian Science: The devil is a lie, a belief in sin, sickness, death. The supposition that there are good and evil spirits is a mistake. Christian Science teaches that "the evil one" is but another name for the first lie and all liars.

Christadelphianism: The devil is not a personal supernatural agent of evil, and in fact there is no such being in existence. The devil is a scriptural manifestation of sin in the flesh in its several phases of manifestations . . . after the style of metaphor which speaks of wisdom as a woman, riches as mammon, and Satan as the god of this world.

The corruption of human society is another element in the Satanic strategy. God's order for human society is clearly stated:

> Let every person be in subjection to the governing authorities. For there is no authority except from God, and those which exist are established by God. Therefore he who resists authority has opposed the ordinance of God; and they who have opposed will receive condemnation upon themselves. [Romans 13:1-2]

In his campaign to undermine the authority of God and tear down the structure of a God-fearing society, the devil incites men to lawlessness and permissiveness. In our day these tendencies have perhaps reached their zenith. Never in human history has lawlessness reached such universal proportions, and in all strata of society. It would seem that today we see the fulfilment of Revelation 12:12: "Woe to the earth and the sea, because the devil has come down to you, having great wrath, knowing that he has only a short time."

A new era of permissiveness has paved the way for moral corruption on an immense scale until even its own devotees are revolted by their own degeneration. The worldwide upsurge in the use of drugs and the alarming increase in alcoholic addiction are all part of his devilish strategy to enslave man to his own passions.

Had Paul lived in our day he could not have drawn a more accurate picture than he paints in 2 Timothy 3:1-5.

In the last days difficult times will come. For men will be lovers of self, lovers of money, boastful, arrogant, revilers, disobedient to parents, ungrateful, unholy, unloving, irreconcilable, malicious gossips, without self-control, brutal, haters of good, treacherous, reckless, conceited, lovers of pleasure rather than lovers of God; holding to a form of godliness, although they have denied its power.

The attitude of the general public to law and enforcement is evidence of the degree to which this stratagem has succeeded. There is more sympathy with the criminal than for the victim. The law enforcement officer generally looks in vain for the support of those he protects.

IDOLATRY AND THE DEVIL

Among heathen peoples of the world, the devil holds almost undisputed sway. And he intends to keep it that way.

Heathendom has been defined by Mildred Cable as

the condition of men and women whose worship is not directed toward God but toward Satan, whose minds Satan darkens. . . . Their development is arrested and their soul entombed. . . . Behind the hideous idol lurks the being to whom all idol worship is directed. And behind the contemplative Buddha presides the prince whose one and only aim is to divert the homage from Him Who alone is entitled to receive it, God the Father, Almighty, Maker of heaven and earth.[3]

Heathen idols and deities are not just figments of the imagination. Heathenism rests on a spiritualistic foundation. The New Testament teaching is that heathen gods such as Apollo, Aphrodite, and Diana were not mere personifications of the powers of nature, but actual demonic forces were behind them.

It is true that the physical idol is nothing in itself and

is devoid of power. But the demons behind them to whom the heathen consciously direct their worship are something very real and powerful. Paul left the Corinthian Christians in no doubt of this.

> What do I mean then? That a thing sacrificed to idols is anything, or that an idol is anything? No, but I say that *the things which the Gentiles sacrifice, they sacrifice to demons, and not to God;* and I do not want you to become sharers in demons. [1 Corinthians 10:19-20, italics added]

To one who accepts the testimony of Scripture, words could not be clearer.

Because he was so convinced of the danger of contact with evil spirits, Paul urged believers to flee from idolatry. Those who worshiped or ate food offered to idols laid themselves open to satanic power. Behind every idol lurks a demon. The Bible traces idolatry to demonic influence and makes worshipers of false gods worshipers of demons. Yet some Christian writers laud the Hindus, for example, for their sublime "oriental consciousness of God," whereas they worship thousands of deities, back of whom is the master mind of Satan. The word *demons* is used of objects of worship, and in idolatry we need to recognize the hidden influence of demons under the control of Satan (Revelation 16:14).

Because of their idolatry and its attendant licentiousness the Canaanites were expelled from Canaan.

The divinely ordered expulsion or extermination of the Canaanites has long been a stumbling block to those to whom the authority of Scripture is not paramount. Why should God make such an uncompromising demand? The religion of the Canaanites was riddled with advanced forms of spiritual wickedness, which in turn induced moral corruption. Their idolatry and corruption had begun to infect God's chosen people and were about to frustrate the purposes of blessing for the whole world, which He planned to achieve through them.

We are told how this leaven was at work in Israel. "He forsook God who make him. . . . They made Him jealous with strange gods; with abominations they provoked Him to anger. *They sacrificed to demons* who were not God" (Deuteronomy 32:15-17).

Israel had been warned of this peril. "Do not defile yourselves by any of these things; for by all these the nations which I am casting out before you have become defiled" (Leviticus 18:24). And again, "Because of these detestable things the LORD your God will drive them out before you" (Deuteronomy 18:12). And what were those abominable practices? Burning sons and daughters as sacrifices; practicing soothsaying, divination, sorcery, spiritism, necromancy.

Their great goddesses Asherah, Astarte, and Anath were violent goddesses of sex and war; and their idolatry involved them in incredible licentiousness and cruelty.

In considering this subject, we should not forget that the Canaanites were not compelled to stay in Palestine and be killed. They had the option to flee. Many did flee and founded flourishing colonies on the shores of the Mediterranean.

Far from being an act of cruelty, the divine command to drive out or destroy the Canaanites was an act of farsighted mercy in the higher interest of the whole human race. It was an act of moral surgery. Removal from Palestine was essential for the preservation of Israel from the contaminating influences of idolatry and its attendant evils.

No cancer patient, whose malignancy has been removed to preserve the healthy tissue from corruption, would charge his benefactor with cruelty because he excised that which would inevitably cause his death. God removed the Canaanites lest they irreparably corrupt the Israelites and infect the whole of humanity with their malignant virus. Was not the Flood a similar act of moral surgery?

STRATEGY WITH BELIEVERS

The most virulent opposition of the devil is directed against the Body of Christ. His fixed purpose is to *annihilate the church or to neutralize its witness.* Because the resurrection has forever removed Christ from his reach, the only way he can now attack Him is through "the Church which is His body."

It did not take him long to show his hand after the church had been instituted at Pentecost. It was *from within* the infant church that Satan launched his first assault. Following Barnabas's sacrificial gift of property, Ananias and Sapphira conspired together to "lie to the Holy Spirit." The record is careful to reveal the source of the temptation that brought such judgment, and the satanic influence that inspired it. "*Why has Satan filled your heart* to lie to the Holy Spirit, and to keep back some of the price of the land?" (Acts 5:1-6). At the very beginning of the dispensation of the Holy Spirit, God vindicated His authority in the church and intervened in salutary judgment when dissimulation and deceit threatened to undermine that body.

"*To keep back some of the price*" is the operative clause. Satan is always at our side to induce us to settle for less than absolute surrender to Christ. He will even encourage the surrender of *much,* but becomes desperately concerned and active when the soul appears to be on the point of yielding *all* to Christ. It is the person who has brought every area of life under the dominion of Christ who poses a serious threat to his kingdom.

When the believer reaches the place of full surrender to the Lordship of Christ, and Satan sees he is determined to follow the Lord at whatever cost, he then moves in to *deflect him from the way of the cross.* Christ's unvarying conditions of discipleship included this: "Whoever does not carry his own cross and come after Me cannot be My disciple" (Luke 14:27). The devil aims to break down this fixed purpose.

When Jesus shared the certainty of His death with the disbelieving disciples, impetuous Peter, doubtless out of real love and loyalty, "began to rebuke Him, saying, 'God forbid it, Lord! This shall never happen to You.' But He turned and said to Peter, 'Get behind Me, Satan! You are a stumbling block to Me; for you are not setting your mind on God's interests, but man's" (Matthew 16:22-24).

Satan will use our own well-meaning friends and relatives to join forces with our weak flesh in an attempt to deflect us from bearing our own cross after Him.

PERSECUTION AND POPULARITY

The adversary's next assault on the infant church came *from without,* in the form of *virulent persecution.* The messengers of the gospel were threatened, arrested, imprisoned, stoned, flogged, tortured, and killed for their loyal witness to Christ. Successive Roman emperors ruthlessly persecuted the law-abiding Christian community. But, like the Israelites, the more they were persecuted, the more they increased.

When he saw this stratagem fail to halt the onward march of the church, Satan switched tactics and endeavored to *smother its witness by according it great popularity.* In that he met with more success. That popularity, which reached its zenith in the reign of the Emperor Constantine, greatly weakened the church.

Through the centuries, Satan has rung the changes on those methods of attack and has often been tragically successful in achieving his objective. Except in a few local situations, however, he failed to annihilate the church. This should be no surprise, for at the very first mention of His church, Jesus stressed its invincibility— not its weaknesses. "Upon this rock I will build My church; and the gates of Hades shall not overpower it" (Matthew 16:18).

Just as he attempted time and again by subtle suggestion and seductive temptation to deflect Jesus from the way of the cross, so the devil designs to lure the disciple from following his Lord along the same road.

DIVISIVE TACTICS

If he cannot destroy the church, Satan aims to discredit it. And he has found many ways in which he can thwart God's purpose through it. One of his most successful gambits has been *to disturb the unity of the church by creating discord and division*. Believers are exhorted to "maintain the unity of the Spirit," that is, the unity that the Spirit has created. The fact is implicit that the unity of the church is continually subject to attack. Satan used this method early in the Christian era and has exploited it ever since.

He works by playing on the prejudices, ambitions, and jealousies of church members. He fosters a spirit of intolerance and suspicion to break the bonds of mutual confidence. He creates parties and factions within churches to fragment them and neutralize their witness. Few attitudes play more into his hands in this area than a critical spirit. Misunderstandings arise very quickly when a censorious spirit is harbored. Satan is thus given a tremendous advantage, which he is not slow to exploit.

He often reserves this form of attack for those he cannot deceive about the teachings of the Word of God, or whom he cannot deflect from doing the will of God. He will cause them to be so ardent in defense of the truth or their own particular interpretation of it, that Christian charity and courtesy are forgotten and give place to intolerance, suspicion, and acrimonious criticism. The battleground shifts from doctrines to personalities.

On the mission field, he causes division among missionaries and within mission groups, creating small splinter groups who are either unable or unwilling to work with other evangelical groups. At the end of World War II there remained only 200 missionaries among the 100 million Japanese. Within a very few years there were 150 different mission *groups,* the majority of them evangelical, but many of them working in isolation. That greatly confused the Japanese. Such unnecessary fragmentation affords our adversary keen delight.

Another stratagem of his is *the subversion of the church through apostasy and heresy.* The church had scarcely been born before the devil began to infiltrate it with emissaries who promulgated false doctrine, especially concerning the Person of Christ. Peter wrote of it in these words:

> But false prophets also arose among the people, just as there will also be false teachers among you, who will secretly introduce destructive heresies, even denying the Master who bought them. . . . And because of them the way of the truth will be maligned. [2 Peter 2:1-2]

Paul indicated the source of that apostasy: "But the Spirit explicity says that in later times some will fall

away from the faith, *paying attention to deceitful spirits and doctrines of demons"* (1 Timothy 4:1, italics
added). What are we to understand by "doctrines of
demons?"

DOCTRINES OF DEMONS

Nowhere are Satan and his servants more ceaselessly
active than in the theological field. He knows well the
liberating and illuminating power of the truth of God.
So He aims to destroy man's confidence in God's Word
and to adulterate His truth.

Paul clearly envisaged this development in his statement, "But the Spirit explicitly says that in later times
some will fall away from the faith, paying attention to
deceitful spirits and doctrines of demons" (1 Timothy
4:1). The apostasy Paul foresaw would be the direct
work of deceitful spirits working through insincere
teachers. *Doctrines of demons* means doctrines taught
by demons—a solemn thought!

In the church at Thyatira were those who had learned
not the deep things of God but "the deep things of
Satan" (Revelation 2:24). In our day we find the same
spirits working through theologians and preachers, using orthodox terminology to inculcate heterodox doctrine. The devil is consistent in his doctrinal emphasis.
He attacks key doctrines. He undermines the inspiration
and authority of Scripture. He denies that Christ is come
in the flesh. He attacks the uniqueness and deity of
Christ. He eliminates the substitutionary element in His
death. He teaches that Christ's resurrection was only
spiritual, whatever that means. He impugns the personality of the Holy Spirit, who unveils his nefarious works,
for it was the Holy Spirit who unveiled Satan's part in
Ananias's lie. There is nothing to fear in a Holy Spirit if

He is only an influence.

Peter further unveiled the satanic strategy in the realm of doctrine:

> There will also be false teachers among you, who will secretly introduce destructive heresies, even denying the Master who bought them. . . . And because of them the way of the truth will be maligned; and in their greed they will exploit you with false words. [2 Peter 2:1-3]

SATAN IN THE PULPIT

Preaching on methods adopted by the devil in attaining his ambition, Donald G. Barnhouse said that one of the simplest and yet most easily detected ruses of Satan is that he gets "ordained" and speaks from Christian pulpits. To support that affirmation, Dr. Barnhouse cited this Scripture:

> For such men are false apostles, deceitful workers, disguising themselves as apostles of Christ. And no wonder, for even Satan disguises himself as an angel of light. Therefore it is not surprising if his servants also disguise themselves as servants of righteousness; whose end shall be according to their deeds. [2 Corinthians 11:13-15][4]

Few will dispute the fact that in thousands of pulpits over the world sermons that deny the central doctrines of the Christian faith are preached every Lord's Day, and in the name of Christianity. Time was when such men would honestly claim to be atheists and leave the church. But in our day, even the "God is dead" theologians were hailed by many churches, ministers, and theological professors as harbingers of new light. And they are still accorded high honor in theological circles.

When Satan can so deceive ministers of the gospel as to promulgate from their Christian pulpits errors that he himself has spawned, he has gained a signal victory. The church's witness is short-circuited and its pretensions are justly exposed to a cynical world's contempt.

Satan will do all in his power to hinder the restoration of a Christian who has failed in life and service. This is illustrated in Zechariah 3.

After the return from the Babylonian exile, God granted Zechariah a symbolical vision. He saw Joshua the high priest about to take up his sacred duties in the now restored Temple. His office was representative, for his function was to represent the whole nation before God.

A trial apparently was in progress in heaven. Joshua stood at the bar. At his right was Satan, the adversary, "to accuse him." To his dismay, Zechariah saw that Joshua was clothed with filthy garments. According to the Mosaic law that utterly disqualified him—and in him the whole nation—not only from fellowship with God, but also for the sacred ministry entrusted to him.

> He showed me Joshua the high priest standing before the angel of the LORD, and Satan standing at his right hand to accuse him. And the LORD said to Satan, "The LORD rebuke you, Satan." [Zechariah 3:1-2]

As the adversary leveled his accusations, Joshua had no answer. Nor had the nation, for the reference to Jerusalem (v. 2) indicated that the accusations of the adversary included the whole nation. It was God's purpose to remove Joshua's filthy garments and clothe him in festal attire. But Satan always prefers to see the believer in defiled garments, and thus powerless to harm the kingdom of darkness.

Note that while neither Joshua nor his people had any answer to Satan's accusations—for they knew them to be all too true—the Judge Himself stepped in, refuted the accusations and rebuked the accuser. Satan always delights to see a saint disqualified because of defilement. But our Advocate delights to remove filthy garments, replace them with the robe of His own righteousness, and give His child a fresh opportunity of service as He did with Joshua.

> Thus saith the LORD of hosts, "If you will walk in My ways, and if you will perform My service, then you will also govern My house and also have charge of My courts, and I will grant you free access among these who are standing here. [Zechariah 3:7]

He also uses the pressures and care of spiritual service to erode the believer's devotional life and thus make him spiritually powerless. He promotes secondary priorities to first place and thus reduces effectiveness. "And the worries of the world, and the deceitfulness of riches, and the desires for other things enter in and choke the word, and it becomes unfruitful" (Mark 4:19).

The apostles faced the problem of perverted priorities very early in their program. With the multiplication of converts, the legitimate social responsibilities of the infant church began to crowd out the more important spiritual ministries. The apostles had the insight to perceive that incipient satanic deflection and announced their determination to put first things first.

> It is not desirable for us to neglect the word of God in order to serve tables. But select from among you, brethren, seven men of good reputation, full of the Spirit and of wisdom, whom we may put in charge of this task. But *we will devote ourselves to prayer, and to the ministry of the word.* [Acts 6:2-3, italics added]

The Christian worker will always be subject to pressure from the adversary to allow his horizontal relationship with his fellow men to take precedence over his vertical relationship with God, and indeed to oust it altogether. That is exactly what is taking place on a worldwide scale in the current emphasis of the ecumenical movement. Not that social action is not authorized in Scripture, but many church leaders have accorded it a priority not given to it in Scripture. Meanwhile billions of soul languish "without God and without hope in the world."

HINDERING MISSIONARY WORK

To prevent the extension of Christ's kingdom, the devil concentrates powerful forces on hindering the missionary enterprise. No sooner had the first two missionaries begun their momentous assignment, than they met Satan-inspired opposition from Elymas, a magician who withstood them. With Spirit-given insight, Paul saw behind Elymas the evil one who had inspired his opposition, and uttered a stinging rebuke:

> Paul, filled with the Holy Spirit, fixed his gaze upon him, and said, . . "You son of the devil, you enemy of all righteousness, will you not cease to make crooked the straight ways of the Lord?" [Acts 13:9-10]

Paul also attributed the repeated frustration of his plans to visit the Thessalonian Christians to satanic activity. "We . . . were all the more eager with great desire to see your face. For we wanted to come to you—I, Paul, more than once—and yet Satan thwarted us" (1 Thessalonians 2:17-18). We cannot attribute all obstructions in our path to satanic activity, but Paul discerned the cloven hoof in those frustrated attempts to build up the church.

The adversary has many arrows in his quiver, as missionary history testifies. He attacks new converts with unbelievable ferocity, especially after they have made a break with their old life at their baptism. He compels a false worship, as in the early church when everyone was faced with the alternative of engaging in emperor worship or suffering terrible consequences, even death. In our times, in Japan during World War II, shrine-worship was compulsory, and the penalty for failing to conform was severe.

He raises antipathy and opposition to the messengers of the gospel in heathen lands and endeavors to secure their expulsion from the country. The "Missionary Go Home" movement, while caused in part by wrong missionary attitudes, was the result of Satan's activity.

He creates apathy towards the missionary obligation of the churches in the sending countries and dries up the springs of Christian liberality.

He prevents young Christians from committing themselves to missionary work by propagating false conceptions of the missionary vocation.

He pressures the missionary into such feverish activity that he becomes worn out in body and in spirit.

Can we say, "We are not ignorant of his devices"?

8

Heavenly Armor

This armour is not like those antiquated suits we are accustomed to look at in the Tower of London or else-where; it is for present use, and has never been improved upon. Modern weapons are out of date in a few years—this armour, never. God does not tell us to look at it, to admire it, but to put it on, for amour is of no use until it is put on. [1]

F. C. Jennings

THE FULL PANOPLY OF GOD

Soldiers of Christ, arise,
And put your armor on,
Strong in the strength which God supplies
Through His eternal Son;
Strong in the Lord of hosts,
And in His mighty power,
Who in the strength of Jesus trusts
Is more than conqueror.

CHARLES WESLEY CAPTURED in that hymn the truth Paul was teaching in Ephesians 6:10-18. Before the Christian soldier dons the whole armor of God, Paul exhorts him to constantly allow himself to be strengthened *in the Lord* and in the strength of *His* might. He takes it for granted that believers possess no inherent power to overcome the unceasing attacks of the evil once. It is useless to have strong armor without if we are weak within. We must experience the divine strengthening as well as put on the divine panoply, as Wesley continues:

> Stand, then, in His great might,
> With all His strength endued;
> And take, to arm you for the fight,
> The panoply of God.

We note four things about this panoply, or armor. First, it is not our armor we are to put on, but *God's*. We have nothing of our own that will afford us sure protection from and victory over our wily adversary. The weapons from our own arsenal are pitifully weak. Only the armor that God supplies will avail. He supplies it freely, but it is for us to take and use.

Second, armor is of value only when we face *an external foe.* It is powerless and utterly ineffective in dealing with the flesh, that traitor within the citadel of man's soul. The only way to deal with the flesh is to mortify it, to count it as dead.

Third, God makes no provision for armor for the back. He expects the soldiers of His army to be on the offensive. God lends no encouragement to us to turn tail and flee from the enemy when the battle grows fierce.

Last, we need the *whole* armor of God. If we put on every piece except one, we leave an Achilles' heel, a vulnerable spot that will enable Satan to gain the initiative and inflict defeat on us. "What boots it at one gate to make defense, and at another to let in the foe?" We learn from Galatians 3:27 that to put on the whole armor of God is the equivalent of nothing less than "putting on Christ." Wesley's hymn warns us:

> Leave no unguarded place,
> No weakness of the soul

> Take every virtue, every grace,
> And fortify the whole.

Paul also emphasised the conflict in which we are engaged is *spiritual* in nature.

> For our struggle is not against flesh and blood, but against the rulers, against the powers, against the world forces of this darkness, against *the spiritual forces of wickedness* in the heavenly places. [6:12, italics added]

The Christian soldier must be alert to see beyond his flesh and blood antagonists the spirits of evil that control them. Behind the men are subtle and powerful demonic powers against whom he must stand.

> That, having all things done,
> And all your conflicts passed,
> You may o'ercome through Christ alone,
> And stand complete at last.

THE PIECES OF ARMOR

THE BELT

The first piece of armor to be buckled on is *the belt of truth*. Paul follows the natural order in which a soldier would put on his armor. It was to the belt that the other pieces of armor were attached, and it held them in place. The belt unified the soldier's whole equipment. From it the sword was suspended. It not only afforded him freedom of movement in conflict, but it also protected his loins.

The truth is the unifying and strengthening factor in the life and experience of the Christian soldier. Was not Satan's first attack on the human race waged in the realm of truth? Did he not impugn the truthfulness of God? "Did God say you shall not eat of the fruit of the garden?" he asked.

And the woman said to the serpent . . . God has said,

"You shall not eat from it or touch it, lest you die." And
the serpent said to the woman, "You surely shall not die!"
[Genesis 3:2-3]

We must be prepared for the father of lies to attack us
in this area of our lives, too. He will tempt us to hypocrisy and insincerity, inciting us to indulge in untruth or
half-truths. Our only security lies in our whole life's
being incircled and held captive by the truth of God. To
that end we must saturate ourselves in the great truths of
God's holiness, righteousness, love, power, and unfail-
ing faithfulness.

Am I ready to embark on this spiritual warfare? Does
God find "truth in the inward parts" in me? Is my heart
sincere, free from guile and hypocrisy? It is God's truth
applied to heart and life that prepares us for warfare.

THE BREASTPLATE

The breastplate of righteousness must be buckled
onto the belt of truth. The function of the breastplate,
which covered the body of the warrior from neck to
thighs, was to protect his vital organs.

Righteousness here is not viewed as an abstract quality, but rather a quality embodied in a holy life, "a clear
conscience toward God and towards men." It is Christ's
righteousness *imputed* to us. But it is more than that. It
is God's righteousness *imparted* and *inworked* in us by
the Holy Spirit, resulting in inner integrity of character.
Where there is no moral rectitude in the life, we have no
defense against the accusations of the adversary. But
when our hearts do not condemn us, we have powerful
armor against his attacks and accusations.

THE SHOES

In all ages, great attention has been paid to *the soldier's footwear.* A soldier who cannot march is disabled

for warfare. Hence the necessity of having our feet shod with the equipment of the gospel of peace. Josephus records that the sandals of the Roman soldier were thickly studded with nails to equip him for long, swift marches. The figure here, then, is of a soldier ready for quick action, the antithesis of lethargy and ease. We have to scale steep mountains in this warfare. We have to make forced marches and must have appropriate footwear.

Paradoxically, this readiness springs from the gospel, which alone brings peace. What message but our gospel brings peace instead of worries, anxieties, and pressures? It is the glory of the good news that it makes the Christian warrior ready and eager to wage warfare with the enemy whose aim it is to destroy the peace of God and man. A heart at peace with God equips him to be perennially ready for gospel witness, even to the uttermost part of the earth.

Do I display constant readiness to share the gospel of peace with others?

THE SHIELD

The Roman *shield* was made of brass covered with leather, oblong in shape and measuring about four feet by two feet, six inches. It afforded protection for the whole body. Similarly *the shield of faith* protects the Christian warrior's whole person. The very name indicates its function as a protection from the flaming missles of doubt and unbelief. Arrows in ancient times were often dipped in pitch. Before they were dispatched they were set afire, and were therefore formidable weapons. Before going into battle, the soldier soaked his leather-covered shield in water. The wet leather quenched the fiery darts, while the brass beneath blunted and deflected the arrow.

Just so, a calm and confident trust in our God effectively extinguishes the arrows tipped with fire from hell as they rain on the shield of our faith.

The tense of the verb does not indicate a mere single act of faith, but a maintained attitude of trust in the power of God to give victory. We are to take no holidays from the attitude of faith, for Satan's temptations are as erratic as lightning. One does not know in what area he will attack next.

Joseph had no idea, when he entered Potiphar's house that morning, that he was about to face the crisis on which his whole life would turn. Indeed, the history of the world changed because of his faithfulness. He was saved by the fact that he had cultivated the *habit* of faith and loyalty to God.

Paul was using the shield of faith when he exclaimed,

> I am convinced that neither death, nor life, nor angels, nor principalities, nor things present, nor things to come, nor powers, nor height, nor depth, nor any other created thing, shall be able to separate us from the love of God, which is in Christ Jesus our Lord. [Romans 8:38-39]

THE HELMET

The helmet of leather or brass, was, of course, to protect the head. It, too, was a weapon of defense. *The helmet of salvation* has special reference to the guarding of the mind, the thought life. Satan's fiery darts are directed at the head as well as at the heart. An unguarded, undisciplined mind makes the Christian warrior an easy prey to unbelieving or defiling thoughts and to other deceptions of the enemy.

The devil fights for control of the mind, hence his

penetration of the education system, of literature, and of the communications media of the world. Paul entertained a fear of the brilliant Corinthians in this regard. "But I am afraid, lest as the serpent deceived Eve by his craftiness, your minds should be led astray from the simplicity and purity of devotion to Christ" (2 Corinthians 11:3).

Note that the armor of God is not physical, but mental and spiritual. The mind is the devil's workshop, hence the necessity to bring "every thought captive to the obedience of Christ" (2 Corinthians 10:5). It is the helmet of salvation that will protect our thought life—salvation experienced and understood. It is not sufficient to have correct definitions of what salvation is. The demons have that knowledge and shudder. It is a salvation that is a present, enjoyed fact of experience that the Word means.

Salvation is a spacious word, embracing the past, the present, and the future. *We have been saved* from the guilt and penalty of past sin. *We are being saved* from the power of sin in the present. *We shall be saved* even from the contaminating presence of sin in the future when Christ returns. The experimental knowledge and enjoyment of "so great salvation," the assurance that it is secure and complete, is a great factor in spiritual warfare.

Am I absolutely convinced that "He is able to save forever those who draw near to God through him?" (Hebrews 7:25). If I allow a fiery dart of doubt of that fact to find lodging in my mind, a conflagration will break out in the inflammable material of the old nature, and I will be disqualified for aggressive warfare against the powers of darkness.

THE SWORD

The Roman sword was short, strong, and sharp, eminently suited for aggressive, hand to hand fighting. The Christian warrior is to *take,* to accept from the hand of the Issuing Officer, *the sword of the Spirit* as an offensive as well as a defensive weapon.

Children are often taught the catchy chorus:

> Draw your swords, use your swords,
> For the battle is the Lord's.

The idea behind the chorus is clear and legitimate, but the words themselves harbor a misconception. The Bible is not *our* sword. It is *the sword of the Spirit, which is the Word of God.* Apart from their application to the heart and mind by the Holy Spirit, the words printed in the Bible are no more potent than words printed in any other book, except that they are truth without error. The Word of God proclaimed in the power of the Spirit is powerful. But it is the Spirit's presence in the Word that makes it a living Word.

Many of us know from experience that it is quite possible for the Word to be proclaimed by a preacher in perfectly orthodox terms, yet for it to be devoid of spiritual power. It is only when the sword is wielded by the Holy Spirit that it is powerful and effective. When spoken merely in human power and wisdom, that very Word of God can actually have a deadening effect. "The letter killeth, but the Spirit giveth life." How dependent, then, we should be on the Holy Spirit in our witness and preaching, for it is He who imparts its dynamic and makes it

> living and active and sharper than any two-edged sword,
> and piercing as far as the division of soul and spirit, of
> both joints and marrow, and able to judge the thoughts

and intentions of the heart. [Hebrews 4:12]

Cromwell's Ironsides were reputed to have fought with a Bible in one hand and a sword in the other—an apt picture of the ideal Christian warrior. It is when the Holy Spirit is able to wield this weapon through us that we become instruments in the defeat of the devil. Was not this the secret of the victory of the Spirit-filled and Word-filled Christ in the wilderness temptation?

If we do not learn the use of the sword of the Spirit, we are to all intents and purposes rendered noncombatant. Am I, then, by study and by practicing, skilful in the use of the sword of the Spirit?

ALL-PRAYER

The last piece of armor we must appropriate is *the weapon of all-prayer.* "With all prayer and petition pray at all times *in the Spirit,* and with this in view, be on the alert with all perseverance and petition for all the saints" (Ephesians 6:18, italics added).

This last weapon imparts effectiveness to all the others. It undergirds them all and transforms the consciously weak warrior into an overcomer. We can hope to overcome our wily, malignant adversary only by this type of praying—persistent, alert, intense, believing. Are we expert in this art? It is prayer "in the Spirit" that receives the answer. Prayer offered in the sphere of the Spirit and in the power of the Spirit. It is prayer prompted by the Spirit and originating in His mind. Prayer that originates only in benevolent human desires inflicts no damage on the kingdom of Satan.

It is unselfish prayer—"making supplication for all the saints." It is "all-prayer"—prayer in all places, on all occasions, for people of every nation and station in life. It is *prayer without ceasing.* Only thus can the Christian soldier maintain the lines of communication with his Divine Commander.

When "we do not know how to pray as we ought," the Spirit is there to help us in our weakness, and to instruct us in what is the will of God. He "intercedes for the saints according to the will of God," so every Spirit-inspired prayer will have its answer (Romans 8:26-27). What an invincible piece of armor is this! Am I wearing it?

> Gird thy heavenly armor on,
> Wear it every night and day,
> Ambushed lies the Evil one;
> Watch and pray.
> > Charlotte Elliot

9

Delegated Authority

Among the high privileges that spring from the believer's exalted position, seated in the heavenlies in Christ, the highest no doubt has to do with what may be called 'delegated authority.' The believer commands and it is done. In the Name of Jesus the believer exercises 'executive authority'—he commands the mountains to be moved and to be cast into the sea, and if he doubts not in his heart it is done.

It will not do to wave the matter aside and say, but Jesus was not talking about mountains, it is just a figure of speech! He is certainly referring to mountains of a different order. But saying that, we have only augmented the problem. These are the mountains as all Christian workers know, hardest to move. Science can take care of the former, but who can move the mountains of satanic oppression that are upon the nations and peoples today? Who will remove the mountains of satanic machination interfering with God's Church?[1]

F. J. Huegel

THE CHRISTIAN WARRIOR needs not only armor without but also power and authority within. In the New Testament two different Greek words are translated by the one English word "power"—for example, "Behold I give unto you power *(exousia)* to tread on serpents and scorpi-

ons, and over all the power *(dunamis)* of the enemy"
(Luke 10:18 KJV).* The Greek word *dunamis* is used to
convey the idea of *inherent* power, as distinct from *exousia,* which means *delegated* power or authority.

CHRIST'S STRIKING EXAMPLE

Dunamis, or inherent power, is never predicated of
our Lord by the evangelists, nor do they represent Him
as exercising it, even though He possessed it. The only
occasion when both words were used of Him is in Luke
4:36. "What is this message? For with authority and power He commands the unclean spirits, and they come
out." But it should be noted that was only the conclusion of the spectators, not the declaration of the inspired
evangelists. It is always *exousia* that they attributed to
Him, for example, "All authority *(exousia)* has been giv-
en to Me in heaven and on earth" (Matthew 28:18).

That striking fact would seem to indicate that, though
Son of God and Son of Man, our Lord so completely
subjected Himself to the limitations of our humanity
that in all His mighty works He was not exhibiting His
own inherent power but only exercising the authority
He received from His Father. It was not that He did not
possess infinite power, but He refrained from using it.

There is much encouragement for us here. When we
read of Christ's many wonderful works and the power He
displayed in every realm, we are inclined to say, "Yes,
but He had the advantage of being the Son of God with
all that involves. I am only a weak man. It doesn't help
me much in my battling with Satan and sin to tell me
that He possessed power I do not possess. He had re-

---

*King James Version.

sources available to Him that are not at my disposal."

That just is not so. The word used of Him in His working is *exousia,* authority bestowed on Him by Another, not *dunamis,* inherent power. The power He exercised was delegated to Him and received continuously from the Father. Christ did not exercise independently the sovereign power that was His as Son of God. His miracles were performed in the same way as those of His disciples, not by innate divine power. Although He never emptied Himself of His deity, He never drew on His divine power but depended on the power of the Holy Spirit indwelling His humanity. He received His power from the Father in response to continuing faith.

So instead of being discouraged by the fact that He was the Son of God and therefore possessed divine power not available to us, we have strong reason for encouragement. While possessing such power, He refused to use it and was content to exercise only such power as the Father was pleased to delegate to Him.

The traffic policeman on duty does not have much *power.* Any car could knock him over and kill him in a moment. But he has considerable *authority.* Thousands of drivers respect the authority that has been delegated to him, for they know that the power of the state is behind him. When we exercise our delegated authority over Satan and the powers of darkness, all the power of God is behind us. When we exercise our God-given authority, Christ's mighty *power* is released and is available to us.

THE PRAYER OF AUTHORITY

Within the ministry of prayer, there may be contrasting spiritual activity. Our prayers may be the expression of a calm restful faith, as in, "Ask, and it shall be given to you" (Matthew 7:7). Or it may find expression in tense spiritual conflict, as when Paul prayed for the Colossian Christians: "I want you to know how great a struggle I have on your behalf" (Colossians 2:1). We wrestle against rulers and powers (Ephesians 6:12). It is the latter type of praying that seems largely foreign to Christians today.

Jesus was no stranger to that type of praying, and He gave this graphic pictorial representation of the reality of prayer warfare and of praying with authority:

> But if I cast out demons by the Spirit of God, then the kingdom of God has come upon you. Or how can anyone enter the strong man's house and carry off his property, unless he first binds the strong man. And then he will plunder his house. [Matthew 12:28-29]
>
> When a strong man, fully armed, guards his own homestead, his possessions are undisturbed; but when someone stronger than he attacks him and overpowers him, he takes away from him all his armor on which he had relied, and distributes his plunder. [Luke 11:21-22]

Thus trenchantly Jesus refuted the absurd charge of the Pharisees that He was exorcising demons by the power of the prince of demons. As though the devil would be naive enough to destroy his own kingdom! Jesus pointed out that His casting out of demons evidenced His mastery of Satan, not His subservience to him.

THE STRONG MAN

The strong man fully armed keeps his homestead and his possessions only until a man stronger than he overcomes him and takes them. The strong man is obviously the devil, whose power over the souls and minds of men is mighty, though limited. The One "stronger than he" is none other than the Lamb, because of whose blood we can overcome the powers of darkness (Revelation 12:11).

The Lamb is engaged in deathless conflict with *"the strong man,"* and He will not rest until he is overcome, his palace despoiled, and his captives released. In this conflict between rival sovereigns and kingdoms, the intercessor fulfills an important role. His prayers will be fully effective only if he has a vivid sense of the completeness of the victory Christ gained over the devil at Calvary and knows how to exploit that victory.

It was the discovery of the aggressive aspect of prayer that turned defeat into victory in the experience of James O. Fraser, apostle to the Lisu people of southwest China. He had worked for five years with great devotion and self-sacrifice, but with little to show for it. Not only was he discouraged in his work, but also he had almost reached the point of desperation in his inner experience. Deliverance and blessing came through reading an article in a magazine that had been sent to him. Here is his own account:

> What it showed to me was that deliverance from the power of the evil one comes through definite resistance on the ground of the cross. I had found that much spiritual teaching one hears does not seem to work. My apprehension at any rate of other aspects of truth had broken down.
>
> The passive side of leaving everything to the Lord Jesus as our life, while blessedly true, was not all that was needed just then. . . . We need different truth at different times. *Definite resistance on the ground of the cross* was what brought me light, for I found that it worked. I found that I *could* have victory in the spiritual realm whenever I wanted it. . . . One had to learn gradually

how to use this new found weapon of resistance.[2]

An engineer by profession, James O. Fraser was always interested in seeing things work. And as he began to apply this truth, so new to him, he was thrilled to find he had not been misled. The longed-for blessing was poured out on his loved Lisu, first a trickle, then a mighty torrent.

FIRST BIND—THEN PLUNDER

Here is the Lord's prescription for victory. We must bind the strong man before we can plunder his goods. Are we careful to observe this order, or have we been trying, unsuccessfully, to plunder his house while he is still unfettered? If so, small wonder that he has snatched back souls we have endeavored to deliver from his clutches. It is that heartbreaking experience that has discouraged so many missionaries. They have seen people make profession of faith, seen them take some faltering steps forward, and then have watched them sucked back into the vortex of heathenism. Too many of our prayers are just the sincere and repeated offering of an earnest petition rather than what Jesus termed "binding the strong man." It is more often the prayer of hope than the prayer of faith, and God is not pledged to answer the prayer of hope.

Think of this concept as it applied to the Lord Himself. In addition to many minor ones, He had three great encounters with the devil—in the wilderness, in Gethsemane, at Calvary. The temptations in the wilderness He met and overcame through the skilful use of the sword of the Spirit. Vanquished, the devil left Him for a season. Because of that total victory Jesus was able to confidently affirm, "The ruler of the world is coming, and he has nothing in Me" (John 14:30).

His next major encounter with the devil was at Gethsemane. So intense and agonizing was His conflict with the powers of darkness that, contrary to nature, instead of rushing to the support of His breaking heart, the blood forced its way through His pores. How did He triumph over Satan on this occasion? By merging His will in the will of His Father. Note the progression in His prayers:

> He knelt down and began to pray, saying, "Father, if Thou art willing, remove this cup from Me; yet *not My will, but Thine* be done." [Luke 22:41-42, italics added]
>
> He went away again a second time and prayed, saying, "My Father, if this cannot pass away unless I drink it, *Thy will be done.*" [Matthew 26:42, italics added]

There is no mention of His will in the second prayer. The shrinking of the human will evidenced in the first petition had been lost in glad acceptance of the Father's will. There was no longer, *My will* and *Thy will,* but only *Thy will.* He was now able to cry in exultation, "The cup which the Father has given Me, shall I not drink it?" (John 18:11).

Thus Satan suffered another shattering defeat at the hands of the man Christ Jesus, who refused to move from complete acceptance of His Father's will, though He knew it meant death on a cross. With us, too, acceptance of the will of God is an essential prelude to victory.

The complete and final defeat of the devil was consummated at Golgotha, where Christ triumphed over him by His death. "And the hostile princes and rulers He shook off from Himself and boldly displayed them as His conquests, when by the Cross He triumphed over them" (Colossians 2:15, Weymouth). A major purpose of His incarnation was "that through death He might render

powerless [destroy] him who had the power of death,
that is, the devil" (Hebrews 2:14).

"Destroy" in the latter verse involves the same idea as
the command to *bind* the strong man. Christ has destroyed and bound the devil and thus rendered him powerless. As members of His Body we may share His victory,
for His victory is ours.

POTENTIAL AND ACTUAL VICTORY

The practical question arises, How does victory over
Satan become actual and operative in personal life and
practical service? It is not sufficient to know that on the
cross Christ potentially delivered us from Satan's power,
if he still exercises his power over us and holds us captive to sin. The potential must be translated into the
actual. That is done only when we personally and definitely exercise the spiritual authority Christ has given to
us.

When the seventy returned radiant from their tour of
witness, rejoicing that even the demons were subject to
them, Jesus made an amazing statement, the full significance of which is seldom realized "I was watching Satan
fall from heaven like lightning. Behold, *I have given
you authority . . . over all the power of the enemy*"
(Luke 10:18-19, italics added). And we are in a no less
privileged position than those early disciples.

In that utterance, Jesus linked that delegation to His
disciples of authority over *all* the power of the enemy—
an authority they could use in any situation and at any
time—with the overthrow of the devil. As they exercised the authority, they found that it worked, and even
demons were subject to them. "In My name"—that is, by
My authority—"they will cast out demons" (Mark

16:17). Similarly, by using Christ's authority, we may bind Satan, render him powerless, and then confidently plunder his palace.

Jesus was well-known to the demons. "I recognize Jesus," was the declaration of the evil spirit (Acts 19:15). "I know who You are—the Holy One of God" (Mark 1:24). For thirty years they had watched His life and knew they had no hold over Him, and they respected His authority. Are our prayers effectual in binding the strong man, or does he laugh at our puny attempts to spoil his house?

In his *Apology*, addressed to the rulers of the Roman Empire, Tertullian, the early church Father, made this statement:

> All the authority and power we have over them (evil spirits) is from our naming the Name of Christ, and recalling to their memory the woes with which God threatens them at the hand of Christ their Judge, and which they expect one day to overtake them. Fearing Christ in God and God in Christ, they become subject to the servants of God and Christ. So at one touch and breathing, overwhelmed by the thought and realization of those judgment fires, they leave at our command the bodies they have entered, unwilling and distressed, and before your very eyes put to an open shame.[3]

Why did the father of the demon-possessed boy lament over the powerlessness of the disciples, "I brought him to Your disciples, and they could not cure him"? (Matthew 17:16,20). "Because of the littleness of your faith," Jesus said. They had no vital faith in the authority He had given them, and their unbelief had paralyzed them.

When we find ourselves involved in a situation for

which our human power is totally inadequate, it is for us, making use of Christ's authority, to claim the victory He won on the cross, and maintain the stand of faith until the victory becomes manifest in our own situation. This is what "fighting the good fight of faith" means.

God taught that lesson to James O. Fraser as, with a deepening conviction begotten by the Holy Spirit, he claimed in prayer more than a hundred Lisu families for Christ. He wrote:

> Satan's tactics seem to be as follows. He will first of all oppose our breaking through to the place of faith, for it is an authoritative "notice to quit." He does not so much mind formal, rambling prayers, for they do not hurt him much. That is why it is so difficult to attain to a definite faith in God for a definite subject. We often have to strive and wrestle in prayer, before we attain this quiet restful faith. And until we break right through and *join hands with God,* we have not attained to real faith at all. However, once we attain to a *real faith,* all the forces of hell are impotent to annul it. . . . The real battle begins when the prayer of faith is offered.[4]

By making use of Christ's authority, and participating in His victory, we can be instrumental in binding "the strong man" in any given spiritual situation. Only then will we be in a position to spoil his goods and deliver his captives.

> Why should I fear the darkest hour,
> Or tremble at the Tempter's power?
> Jesus vouchsafes to be my power.
>
> Against me earth and hell combine,
> But on my side is power divine,
> Jesus is all, and He is mine.
>   John Newton

10

Overthrow and Doom

The death of our Lord Jesus Christ destroyed—brought to nought—'him that had the power of death, that is the devil.' The word 'destroy' has no suspicion of any such meaning as annihilation but rather that of rendering harmless, useless, worthless. Thus the Lord made a public example of Satan, and immediately proved the decline of Satan's power by taking the keys with which Satan pretended to some authority over the righteous spirits and, entering among them until the three days and nights should be accomplished, announced the freeing of those who had been detained.[1]

Donald G. Barnhouse

WHILE WE MUST NOT UNDERESTIMATE the terrible might, power, and malignity of our adversary, we must be careful not to fall into the opposite error and overestimate it. Fear can paralyze.

> And were this world all devils o'er.
> And watching to devour us,
> We lay it not to heart so sore;
> Not they can overpower us.
> And let the prince of ill
> Look grim as e'er he will,
> He harms us not a whit;
> For why, his doom is writ;

A word shall quickly slay him'.
Martin Luther
(Trans. Thomas Carlyle)

Nowhere does Scripture ascribe to him the divine attributes of omniscience, omnipotence, or omnipresence. The fact that he is a created being means that his power is limited. A quaint preacher asked the question, "Is Satan omnipresent? No, but he is very spry. Is he bound? Yes, but with a rather loose rope." Fortunately he can be in only one place at one time. When he was tempting Christ in the wilderness, the rest of the world was spared his *personal* presence and attention. However, through his vast host of followers he is able to achieve a "limited omnipresence."

Then, too, any power and authority he wields is not inherent, but derived from God. "There is no authority except from God, and those which exist are established by God" (Romans 13:1). And that includes the devil. In his testing of Job, he could go only as far as God gave him permission. He could afflict Job's body with loathsome disease, but he was powerless to take his life. "So the Lord said to Satan, 'Behold, he is in your power, only spare his life'" (Job 2:6).

Although Scripture recognizes him as "the god of this world," the devil is not supreme, and the restraining hand of God is upon him. Even in the matter of temptation he does not have a free hand. "God is faithful, who will not allow you to be tempted beyond what you are able" (1 Corinthians 10:13).

Contrary to popular conception, there is nothing in Scripture to indicate that he is able to foretell the future infallibly. He has to gather his information as we do, but he has the advantage of highly organized hosts of evil but obedient servants at his call. "Declare the things that are going to come afterward, that we may know that you are gods," was Isaiah's challenge (Isaiah 41:23).

Repeatedly the gospels record that the devil moved the enemies of our Lord to arrest or kill Him, but they were utterly powerless to do so until His hour had come. We are completely safe from Satan's power while we are walking in the light with our Lord. We are encouraged to be "in nothing terrified" by our adversaries (Philippians 1:28, KJV), for "greater is He that is in you than he that is in the world" (1 John 4:4). Nothing he can do can separate us from the love of God in Christ (Romans 8:38-39). F. C. Jennings wrote:

> Over all His own who walk dependently upon Him, the Lord throws His protecting shield. Around each one is the hedge that Satan found it impossible to pierce in Job's case, till divine love saw it good even for Job's sake to give that permission. And this is a very great mercy. The child of God need never be distressed by any of these mysterious phenomena that are now engaging the attention of even the leaders of mankind.[2]

We may say then that Satan's power is not inherent but delegated. It is not unlimited but controlled. It is not invincible but shattered (Luke 11:21-22). It is not triumphant but doomed (Revelation 20:2-3).

> Jesus is stronger than Satan and sin,
>   Satan to Jesus must bow;
> Therefore I triumph without and within
>   Jesus saves me now.
>   Author Unknown

CHRIST'S DEFEAT OF SATAN

Any hope the believer has of being an overcomer in the truceless warfare against Satan and his hosts must lie outside himself. He has no internal resources to enable

him to meet and defeat his experienced and wily adversary.

> With force of arms we nothing can,
>   Full soon were we down-ridden;
> But for us fights the proper Man,
>   Whom God Himself hath bidden.
>   Ask ye who is this same?
>   Christ Jesus is His name,
>   The Lord Sabaoth's Son
>   He and no other one
> Shall conquer in the battle.
>   Martin Luther
>   (Trans. Thomas Carlyle)

His only hope is in laying hold of the victory gained
over him by Christ, first in the wilderness and finally on
His cross. That victory was foreshadowed and is affirmed
in Scripture:

> The Son of God appeared for this purpose, that He
> might destroy the works of the devil. [1 John 3:8]
> And He [Jesus] said to them, "I was watching Satan fall
> from heaven like lightning. Behold, I have given you
> authority . . . over all the power of the enemy." [Luke
> 10:18-19]
> When He had disarmed the rulers and authorities, He
> made a public display of them, having triumphed over
> them through Him. [Colossians 2:15]

Those and many other passages attest the stunning
defeat the Lord inflicted on Satan at the cross. It was
there that the seed of the woman bruised and mortally
wounded Satan's head, though He had His heel bruised
in the conflict. The point is that a wound in the head is
mortal, but the heel is not a vital spot. He partook of our
human nature, "that through death He might render
powerless him who had the power of death, that is, the

devil" (Hebrews 2:14).

Since Calvary, the accuser can never again charge the believer with his sin before the throne of God. Since then the vaunted power of the usurper is only an empty show. We remain under his power only because we either do not know or do not use the authority over the powers of darkness that our victorious Lord has delegated to us. He has broken into the strong man's palace and robbed him of his prey (Mark 3:27).

A VANQUISHED FOE

The believer who abides in Christ need entertain no fear of the devil, but should always regard him as already defeated and overcome. Note the tense of the verb in Luke 10:19, "I have given you authority . . . over all the power of the enemy." That is not a *promise* to be claimed from God. It is a statement of fact from the lips of Christ to be believed and acted upon. It denotes the present result of a past action. Once we are set free from Satan's chains, it is for us to exercise our divinely bestowed authority to bind the strong man and plunder his house.

Colossians 2:15 is a key verse to reveal the completeness of our Lord's victory over Satan. "When He disarmed the rulers and authorities, He made a public display of them." Paul had (in the previous verse) referred to the law as an impersonal accuser of the believer (v. 14). Now he names his personal accusers. We have already seen that Satan is the arch-accuser of the saints who seduces men into sin, then accuses them of the very sin that he had incited. As one old Puritan put it, "The devil seduces the Christian into sin, and then lays his brats at the Christian's door."

When Paul wrote this letter, the Colossian Christians

were in the midst of a sinister and subtle attack from the powers of darkness. Paul brought strength and encouragement to them from the fact that, powerful though those forces were, God had disarmed and defeated them through the sacrifice of His Son, who is the Head of the church, as well as the Creator of all authority (1:16; 2:10). He triumphed over Satan in the wilderness and returned in the power of the Spirit (Luke 4:1-14). By His death on Calvary He bound "a strong man fully armed" and took away from him "his armor on which he had relied, and distributes his plunder" (Luke 11:21-22).

By His vicarious death and victorious resurrection, Christ once and for all answered every charge or accusation that Satan could bring against the child of God. That truth caused Paul to break out into his triumphant questions: "Who will bring a charge against God's elect? . . who is the one who condemns?" (Romans 8:33-34). That truth inspired John's ringing declaration: "Now the salvation, and the power, and the kingdom of our God and the authority of His Christ have come, for the accuser of our brethren has been thrown down, who accuses them before our God day and night" (Revelation 12:10).

> I hear the Accuser roar
> Of evils I have done,
> I know them all and thousands more,
> Jehovah findeth none.
>
> Author Unknown

Paul further expounds Christ's victory over Satan through the illustration of the triumphal march of a victorious Roman general returning after a triumphant campaign. His reward was to march his army through the streets of Rome, leading behind him the captive, weaponless kings and peoples he had conquered. He boldly displayed them as his conquests. That is the picture in Colossians 2:15. God made a public example and exposed to public disgrace the evil principalities and powers, showing to all that the victory of Calvary had disarmed them and left them impotent. Satan and his hosts have only as much power over the believer as He allows them to have. For did not Christ say, "Behold I give you power over *all* the power of the enemy?" Their power over mankind is forever broken. Christ's victory over Satan is our victory over Satan, and it is complete.

The Antichrist

Calvary also spelled the doom of the Antichrist. No treatment of our theme would be complete without some reference to one who is the second person of the satanic trinity. The word "antichrist" is found only in the letters of John.

"Children, it is the last hour; and just as you heard that antichrist is coming, even now many antichrists have arisen; from this we know that it is the last hour. They went out from us, but they were not really of us" (1 John 2:18-19).

"This is the antichrist, the one who denies the Father and the Son" (1 John 2:22).

"Every spirit that confesses that Jesus Christ has come in the flesh is from God; and every spirit that does not confess Jesus is not from God; and this is the spirit of the antichrist, of which you have heard that it is coming, and now it is already in the world" (1 John 4:23).

"For many deceivers have gone out into the world, those who do not acknowledge Jesus Christ as coming in the flesh. This is the deceiver and the antichrist" (2 John 7).

The word "antichrist" means simply *opposed to Christ* and can refer equally to a system or a person. John appears to use it in three senses: (a) a spirit or attitude (1 John 4:3); (b) the antichrists, plural (1 John 2:18; 2 John 7); (c) a person (1 John 2:18).

Harold J. Ockenga expressed the view of many when he said that the word *antichrist* describes any anti-Christian system of thinking or acting, but will represent an *apotheosis* in an individual expressing this anti-Christian teaching and tendency at the end time.[3]

Speaking in general terms, an antichrist is a movement or person that opposes Christ as Head of the church and Lord of creation. Such anti-Christian movements have existed ever since the birth of the church, and antichrist exists in every anti-Christian philosophy.

Augustine, and many both before and since, have identified John's *antichrist* with Paul's *man of sin* or *man of lawlessness* (2 Thessalonians 2:3). That this devil's messiah is a human being is attested by the fact that he, like Christ, will have his *parousia* (2 Thessalonians 2:9) and his *apocalypse* (2 Thessalonians 2:8). The early church Fathers expected a sinister and ominous figure to arise who would be motivated and actuated by Satan. "Whose coming is in accord with the activity of Satan, with all power and signs and false wonders" (2 Thessalonians 2:9). It would be difficult to match that language with an impersonal force or movement.

Through the ages there have been many attempts to name the one who would fill the sum of all antichrists who had preceded him—Nero, Alexander, Napoleon, Hitler, all of whom partook of some of his characteristics. But there are many more features yet to be fulfilled.

The Scriptures foreshadow a tremendous climax to the conflict of the ages. The supreme challenge of Satan and his hosts still lies in the future, and it will be headed by this "man of lawlessness." The world will be engulfed in a holocaust of unimaginable horror.

The issue is certain. The antichrist's destiny is enshrined in one of his names, "the son of destruction, who opposes and exalts himself above every so-called god or object of worship, so that he takes his seat in the temple of God, displaying himself as being God" (2 Thessalonians 2:3-4). He is a lost soul fighting a lost cause, for "the Lord will slay [him] with the breath of His mouth and bring [him] to an end by the appearance of His coming" (2 Thessalonians 2:8).

The execution of the final sentence is recorded in vivid and awesome terms: "And the beast . . . and . . . the false prophet . . . were thrown alive into the lake of fire which burns with brimstone" (Revelation 19:20).

11

Invincible Weapons

Satan cannot stand an exposition of the blood of Christ. He turns pale at every view of Calvary. The flowing wounds are the signal of his retreat. A heart besprinkled with the blood is holy ground, on which he not only dares not tread, but he dreads and trembles and cowers in the presence of the blood-besprinkled warrior.

A clear-ringing word of testimony to the power of that blood he fears more than the attack of a legion of archangels. It is like the charge of an irresistible phalanx which bears everything down before it. It is the blood applied, and testimony to its application, the martyr witness in life and by tongue of the power of that blood is more a barrier to Satan than a wall of fire.[1]

Edward M. Bounds

"THERE WAS WAR IN HEAVEN, Michael and his angels waging war with the dragon. And the dragon and his angels waged war, and they were not strong enough" (Revelation 12:7-8).

As we saw in our study of the Christian's armor, the weapons he uses in the unseen battle between God and Satan are spiritual, not material. "For though we walk in the flesh, we do not war according to the flesh, for the weapons of our warfare are not of the flesh, but divinely powerful for the destruction of fortresses" (2 Corinthians 10:3-4).

The war begun in heaven becomes evident on earth. "The devil has come down to you, having great wrath, knowing that he has only a short time" (Rev. 12:12). With the shortening of his time, the devil's anger increases. May not that be the explanation of the incredible intensity of satanic activity in the world today? No part of the world, however remote, is exempt from the revolutionary pressures of our day.

Before detailing three invincible spiritual weapons at our disposal in our spiritual warfare, a loud voice from heaven announces:

> Now the salvation, and the power, and the kingdom of our God and the authority of His Christ have come, for the accuser of our brethren has been thrown down, who accuses them before our God day and night. And they overcame him. [12:10]

And who are those conquerors? The weak, failing men whom the devil has been accusing!

We have already studied some of our weapons of war in the chapter on the Christian's armor. But a variety of figures of speech are necessary to explain adequately the way of victory in this many-sided warfare. We are now introduced to three other spiritual weapons. "They overcame him because of the blood of the Lamb and because of the word of their testimony, and they did not love their life even to death" (12:11).

THE JUDICIAL WEAPON

"The blood of the Lamb"—this weapon derives its potency from Calvary. We cannot emphasize too strongly that the secret of victory over Satan and sin lies not in our inherent powers but in our union with Christ in His

victorious death and resurrection.

The phrase *the blood of the Lamb* is not a kind of magic charm, a ritual that we import into sermon or prayer to attest to our orthodoxy or to secure supernatural results. It is not a formula to be credulously mumbled, nor is it a parroting of mystical words. It is the expression of an intelligent, active, vital faith in Christ, the Lamb of God, who by the shedding of His blood, bruised Satan's head and utterly defeated him.

This is one of the most pregnant and luminous phrases in Scripture. In five words, *the blood of the Lamb,* are concentrated all the virtue and value of Christ's mediatorial work. Blood is life in solution. The life of the Lamb of God, violently shed by sinful men at the instigation of the devil, was voluntarily laid down. But He rose from the dead and ascended to God's right hand by virtue of His own blood, which now becomes the ground of our victory.

Note that the *by* (KJV) in this phrase connotes "because of," not "by means of." Because He broke the power of sin and Satan by shedding His blood, we who are united with Him may share His victory. We are now to regard Satan as already defeated and to claim Christ's victory over him as our own. Satan has no counterweapon to the blood of the Lamb.

So then, when in prayer we plead the blood of the Lamb, we are really saying that our faith is resting for victory over Satan and sin upon all that Christ achieved for us by His vicarious death and victorious resurrection. That is our first weapon of offense.

THE EVIDENTIAL WEAPON

"The word of their testimony." The exercise of faith in the death of Christ is to be followed by witness to His

living and powerful Word. It is not absolutely clear
whether the reference is to the Word to which they bore
testimony or to the testimony itself. Probably both are
included, for any testimony that is not Bible-based is
powerless to achieve spiritual results. Grounded in the
Word of God, our testimony becomes a sword in the
Spirit's hand.

It is not argument or logic or denunciation, but testimony that silences the devil. The Word of Christ and His
apostles, tested in experience, becomes testimony to us.
The Word in the memory alone is not sufficient for warfare with Satan.

THE SACRIFICIAL WEAPON

"They did not love their life even to death." They
held their lives cheap. The Greek word for "testimony"
in this verse is that from which we derive our word
"martyr." The inference is obvious.

This third weapon is not to be directed at the enemy
as are the first two. It is a sword that we take with both
hands and plunge into our breast. The weapon of testimony of one who has the martyr spirit is mightily effective. To him, life is of secondary importance when com-
pared with the outcome of the battle and the victory of
his Lord. His supreme concern is to see Satan defeated
and Christ victorious, even if his life is sacrificed in the
process. He regards himself as expendable.

In this our Lord set a shining example to His followers. The sacrifice of His life did not begin at Calvary or
even at Bethlehem. He was "the Lamb slain from the
foundation of the world." The word of our testimony
will be sterile unless we too tread the way of the cross.
Yet is not this martyr spirit, this spirit of self sacrifice,
largely absent from contemporary Christianity? Is this, in

part, why the church makes so minimal an impact on society?

"They overcame him." Here is a note of undefeatable optimism. Had Jesus not said, "Upon this rock I will build My church; and the gates of Hades shall not overpower it?" (Matthew 16:18). Satan's judgment and defeat were secured at Calvary. But until the sentence is executed, we have these invincible weapons:

> We reckon on the victory of Calvary.
> We bear testimony to its conquering power.
> We are willing to lay down life itself for our Lord.

THE POWER OF THE NAME

Another weapon in the hands of the Christian warrior is the name of Christ. One cannot read the story of the triumphs of the early church without noticing the prominence given to the name of Jesus. In our day, but even more in Eastern lands and in Bible times, the name stands for the whole person with all his characteristics, capacities, powers, and resources. A name written on a check transforms it from a worthless piece of paper into one of great value. A simple signature on a document can mean the transfer of property worth millions of dollars. The name is the person.

Our Lord has given us the privilege and right to use His name. "In My name they will cast out demons" (Mark 16:17). "If you ask Me anything *in My name,* I will do it" (John 14:14, italics added).

When we use Christ's name, we acknowledge we are not acting in our own name or authority, but as His personal representatives. The use of the words "in the name of Jesus" in prayer should not be regarded as a kind of incantation or a pious phrase with which to end our prayers. It has power, but only when accompanied by a living faith in the One to whom it belongs.

Paul knew the power of Christ's name, and used it, as Luke records:

> As we were going to the place of prayer, a certain slave-girl having a spirit of divination met us. . . . Paul . . . turned and said to the spirit, "I command you *in the name of Jesus Christ* to come out of her!" And it came out at that very moment. [Acts 16:16-18, italics added]

It is interesting that when the sons of Sceva, Jewish exorcists, presumed to use the very same formula—they "undertook to pronounce the name of the Lord Jesus over those who had evil spirits"—instead of the demon's coming out of him, the demoniac turned on them and overpowered them.

The name of Jesus has power only on the lips of those who own His Lordship and themselves know the victory of Calvary.

> Jesus! the name high over all,
>   In hell, or earth, or sky,
> Angels and men before it fall,
>   And devils fear and fly.
>   Charles Wesley

12

Be Sober! Be Watchful!

Although demonic activity in human history has always been undeniably great since the sin of our first parents exposed mankind to its baneful attacks, yet the full realization and augmentation of its destructive power are reserved for the consummation of the age. Demonism bears a striking relation to the doctrine of the last things; and all classes of mankind, Jew, Gentile and the Church of God will be intimately and vitally affected by the last-day upsurge of evil supernaturalism.[1]

M. F. Unger

"ETERNAL VIGILANCE IS THE PRICE of freedom," a familiar maxim of the political sphere, is not a whit less appropriate in the spiritual realm. The element of surprise—attack without warning—is an important factor in military warfare. "One belligerent must surprise, the other must be surprised," said General Waldemar Erfurth. "Only when the two commanders play these respective roles, will a battle lead to the annihilation of one army."

> Christian, seek not yet repose,
>   Hear thy guardian angel say,
> Thou art in the midst of foes,
>   Watch and pray!
> Principalities and powers
>   Mustering their unseen array,

> Wait for thy unguarded hours,
> Watch and pray!
> Charlotte Elliot

In Gideon's epic victory over the Midianite hordes, the surprise element played a prominent part. With a paltry 300 men, Gideon surprised their 135,000 warriors and annihilated them. Pearl Harbor is another example. But in that case deception was an added factor, for Japan's envoys were seated at the negotiating table at the very moment the attack was launched.

May we suppose that our resourceful adversary will neglect to use this obvious and effective tactic? A cursory review of Bible history demonstrates how often and successfully he employed it. The only effective counterstrategy is the exercise of eternal vigilance.

But to face the attacks of Satan, the believer should always bear in mind that Satan is a created being and therefore is neither omnipotent nor omniscient. His apparent inability to foresee the divine strategy cost him victory in the battle of the cross. "We speak God's wisdom in a mystery, the hidden wisdom," wrote Paul, "which God predestined before the ages to our glory; the wisdom which none of the rulers of this age has understood; for if they had understood it, they would not have crucified the Lord of glory" (1 Corinthians 2:7-8). No commander would knowingly bring about his own destruction.

In his conduct of spiritual warfare, Paul did not neglect the "intelligence service." "We are not ignorant of his designs," he could say. He was not battling a foe of whose strategy and tactics he knew nothing. In his *Principles of War,* James L. Wilson points out that intelligence of the enemy ensures knowing who he is, his intentions, and his methods of operation. The opposing commander gains this information by listening to all the enemy says and reading all he writes.[2]

One of the purposes of this book is to confront the reader with the body of relevant biblical teaching on the subject, so that he will no longer be spiritually illiterate on this crucial theme, and will be able to combat the adversary intelligently.

WATCHFULNESS A DUTY

Twenty times in the New Testament, watchfulness on the part of the Christian is enjoined. In the majority of cases it is Jesus who commands it. Failure to heed His injunction involved the eleven in tragic failure in Gethsemane. Is there no significance in the fact that Jesus placed watching *before* praying in His counsel to them? If we fail to watch, and thus are caught off guard, the result is a foregone conclusion.

On another occasion Jesus said to them, "What I say unto you, I say unto all, Watch!" Although those words had primary reference to watchfulness in view of His return, the warning is no less applicable to our spiritual adversary, the devil.

A review of areas in which a lack of watchfulness can afford the enemy an advantage in achieving his aims can be of profit.

Ignoring his existence or ignorance of his methods and great power gives him an enormous advantage. If we are uncertain whether such an antagonist really exists, or if we do not seriously take him into account, he has a flying start. How many days are there, for example, when we do not give our supreme enemy even so much as a thought? Could you conceive of such a situation in earthly warfare? Let us retake this lost ground. Let us review the past to discover the successful methods of attack he has adopted in our own experience, and set a watch at that point.

Uncontrolled anger will cost a high price in lost territory. "BE ANGRY, AND YET DO NOT SIN; do not let the sun go down on your anger, and do not give the devil an opportunity" (Ephesians 4:26-27). When we allow even justifiable or unselfish anger to simmer for too long, we give the devil an opportunity to defeat us. And how much more so when our anger is self-centered and therefore sinful. Are we watchful in that area?

A resentful or unforgiving spirit concedes yet more territory to our adversary.

> Whom you forgive anything, I forgive also; . . what I have forgiven, if I have forgiven anything, I did it for your sakes in the presence of Christ, *in order that no advantage be taken of us by Satan;* for we are not ignorant of his schemes. [2 Corinthians 2:10-11, italics added]

An unwillingness to forgive gives him another opportunity to overcome us. We are not to yield him an inch. Are we careful to watch our heart attitudes?

A flippant jesting about the devil may sound smart, but really is very foolish. Both Peter and Jude give strong warnings on this point which we should heed. Peter speaks of those who

> despise authority. Daring, self-willed, they do not tremble when they revile angelic majesties, whereas angels who are greater in might and power do not bring a reviling judgment against them before the Lord. [2 Peter 2:10-11]

Jude adds:

> But Michael the archangel, when he disputed with the devil and argued about the body of Moses, did not dare

pronounce against him a railing judgment, but said, "THE
LORD REBUKE YOU." [Jude 9]

Whatever else those mysterious passages mean, they
surely convey a warning against the presumption of su-
perficial Christians who make light of our ancient foe.
The more intelligent and powerful angels refrain from
this folly. The injunction *"Be of sober spirit, be on the
alert.* Your adversary, the devil, prowls about like a roaring lion, seeking someone to devour" is sufficient warning that conflict with the devil is serious business
(1 Peter 5:8).

Being *mismated with unbelievers* is likened by Paul
to Christ being linked with Belial (or Satan), an unthink-
able association. "What harmony has Christ with Belial,
or what has a believer in common with an unbeliever?"
The believer must not tolerate association with unbelievers in their characteristic activities (2 Corinthians
6:15). To do so is an open invitation to the devil. Although the reference here is primarily to marriage, its
scope is wider and includes any voluntary, binding asso-
ciations.

The leaders in the church also need to exercise care in
the appointment of men to hold office, lest they give
vantage ground to the devil, which he will be fast to
exploit. Paul indicates two areas in which special watchfulness must be exercised.

"A bishop [or overseer, as the word may equally be
rendered] must be above reproach, . . . *He must not be a
recent convert,* or he may be puffed up with conceit and
fall into the condemnation of the devil" (1 Timothy 3:6,
author's paraphrase).

Caution here is especially relevant today. In a laudable
desire to gain and retain the interest of young people,
there is a widespread tendency to rush them into activi-

ties or responsibilities for which they do not yet have either the spiritual maturity or experience. It can damage their own spiritual experience and be disastrous for the work of God. By all means, we should give our young people all the responsibility they are qualified to bear. But the Spirit of God indicates there is a spiritual apprenticeship to be served.

"The condemnation of the devil" probably refers to the judgment that the devil incurred as a result of his unholy ambition and pride. The wisdom of this counsel has been demonstrated so often that it needs no emphasis. There is a very real danger in pushing young converts into prominence too early.

Then too, "He must have a good reputation with those outside the church, so that he may not fall into reproach and the snare of the devil" (1 Timothy 3:7). If a potential church officer has a questionable reputation in the world, both he and the church are open to easy attack by the enemy.

UNHOLY CURIOSITY

In this day when morbid curiosity about all aspects of the occult has reached incredible proportions, we would be culpable not to draw attention to the dangers of dabbling in occultism. A rapidly growing range of literature on this subject may easily lure an unwary uninformed person into situations that can have sinister consequences. Scriptural warnings against such unholy curiosity are plentiful and should be taken seriously:

> There shall not be found among you anyone who makes his son or his daughter pass through the fire, one who uses divination, one who practices witchcraft, or one who interprets omens, or a sorcerer, or one who casts a spell, or a medium, or a spiritist, or one who calls up the

dead. For whoever does these things is detestable to the LORD; and because of these detestable things the LORD your God will drive them out before you [Deuteronomy 18:10-12]

Note how exhaustive and comprehensive that command is, and how categorical the prohibition. Those practices have their modern counterparts in the Satanism of today. Asks A. T. Pierson:

Will anyone show us one substantial benefit accruing to the human race from any attempts to invade this forbidden realm, even scientifically, which begins to overbalance the sad wrecks of body and spirit that lie all along the shores of this Mare Tenebrum?

He goes on to add this caution:

To meddle with this awful realm of spirits may bring us under the sway of malignant supernatural agents and forces. Not only God, but wicked spirits wield weapons which, to us, are superhuman and supernatural, because alike beyond our knowledge and control. In Revelation 16:14, the *spirits of demons* are represented as "working miracles." The devil, belonging to created intelligences of the highest order, can sway man by powers which belong to a higher realm; and to dare to invade those hidden precincts is to venture into an unknown territory, and run corresponding risks; risks which are proportionate to the success of the experiments![3]

Be sober! Be watchful!

> Watch, as if on that alone
>   Hung the issues of the day;
> Pray that help may be sent down,
>   Watch and pray.
>   Charlotte Elliot

13

Whom Resist

Submit yourselves therefore to God. Resist the devil and he will flee from you.

There is an order to observe. Submit is Godward. Resist is Satanward. One comes before the other. The Christian who resists the devil must do so in the Spirit. *By that I mean, one cannot think to approach Satan in the flesh and expect him to flee. That is laughable, for Satan controls the flesh. True, he does it by suggestion, but nonetheless he does it. He will not flee from our flesh. He uses it. Satan has no fear of us. To stand up to him* apart from Christ *would only bring out his sense of humour. It would be like an ant crawling atop the railroad tracks to tell a fast-moving train to stop!*

When you submit to someone, you put yourself under their control. This means that we are to approach Satan under the influence of God's Spirit.[1]

C. S. Lovett

FROM TWO PASSAGES OF SCRIPTURE it is clear that the concept of the believer's taking an attitude of resistance to the devil is thoroughly scriptural:

Submit therefore to God. Resist the devil and he will flee from you. [James 4:7]

Humble yourselves therefore under the mighty hand

133

of God . . . be sober, be vigilant; because your adversary the devil, as a roaring lion, walketh about, seeking whom he may devour: *whom resist* steadfast in the faith. [1 Peter 5:8-9, KJV, italics added]

But in both cases the command to resist is linked with cautionary conditions: (a) His resistance must be preceded by an attitude of submission to God. Defeat of the devil will never be accomplished by those who act in independence of Him. (b) It is the humble man, not the arrogant and self-confident man, who can overcome the enemy. (c) It is the man who is steadfast in the faith who overcomes. It is not the exercise of an unstable and vacillating Christian, but one whose feet are firmly planted on the great verities of our faith.

Those cautions cause us to recognize that the one whom we resist is a vastly experienced, powerful antagonist against whom only the power of God will suffice. Unless we are deeply convinced that the devil is already a vanquished foe, we will not be likely to resist him in the way suggested. Do we have this unshakable assurance? It is the *resistance of faith* James and Peter advocate, and where there is faith, doubt is absent. Calvary is the basis of our resistance.

Note the ringing assurances of Scripture: "Since then the children share in flesh and blood, He Himself likewise also partook of the same, that through death He might render powerless him who had the power of death, that is, the devil" (Hebrews 2:14-15). "The Son of God appeared for this purpose, that He might destroy the works of the devil" (1 John 3:8). "When He had disarmed the rulers and authorities, He made a public display of them, having triumphed over them through Him [the cross]" (Colossians 2:15).

With those divine affirmations under our feet, and in dependence on the mighty Spirit of God, we are in a position to do battle with our ancient foe. We will resist the devil only when we know there is adequate power at our disposal for us to successfully resist him. Scripture never counsels us to ignore the devil. But it does tell us never to fear him, for "greater is He who is in you than he who is in the world" (1 John 4:4).

The attitude of believers should be one of determined resistance to the enemy who holds men captive, and of persistent faith in the sufficiency of Christ's victory at Calvary to set at liberty those who are bound.

A woman told her minister she did not believe the truth of James 4:7. "When I resist the devil, he flies at me," she said. The minister unveiled the cause of her problem when he asked her if her life was fully submitted to God. She had to admit that it was not. Only when a life is submitted is divine power operative and the devil will flee.

Donald G. Barnhouse tells of an experience as a young Christian. In a period of struggle he kept crying out to God that He had told His people to resist the devil and he would flee from them; but as he resisted, it seemed the enemy "fled at him." He opened his Bible and put his finger on James 4:7, but no relief came. Finally the voice of God said, "Read the whole verse." He then saw he had been quoting only half the verse. When the whole truth was read, the perspective was quite different.[2] Before we are told to resist the devil, the preceding line is a prerequisite truth: "Submit therefore to God." If we fail to do the submitting, we will fail to see the devil fleeing.

To the assertion that, since Calvary, Satan is a defeated foe, the easy answer may be: "If that is so, why does he appear to be so active in the world today? He seems to be very busy in the world I live in." Colossians 2:15 categorically states: "When He had disarmed the rulers and authorities, He made a public display of them, having triumphed over them through Him."

The context of that victory is stated in the immediate preceding words, "having nailed it to the cross." The cross of Christ marked the absolute defeat, the judgment, of the devil and all allied with him.

But does it not happen in our society that a criminal is judged and sentence passed and announced sometime before it is actually executed? Men sometimes live in "death row" in a prison for years after they have been sentenced. So is it here. For some reason that God deems wise and good, mysterious though it may seem to us, the sentence on the devil is not yet executed. He and his servants are reserved for a last judgment that is still future (1 Corinthians 6:3). He has been granted limited liberty, although his utter defeat has been effected.

In World War II, when the first atomic bomb dropped at Hiroshima, the Japanese were utterly defeated and the Allies gained a final victory. Nevertheless, the fighting continued for some time. In many parts of the world small pockets of resistance were still being mopped up months later. But that did not mean the outcome of the war had not been decided at Hiroshima.

A partial explanation of the continued freedom granted to Satan has been suggested by L. S. Chafer:

> It seems the course of divine wisdom to make a sufficient and final trial of every claim of His adversaries; and when this age with all its developments shall have passed by, every mouth will be stopped, and the whole world and Satan will see their own failure and sin before God. They will stand self-condemned; and nothing could

accomplish this but the testing, by actual trial, of all the self-sufficient claims of Satan and man. . . . Though the day of execution is, in the purpose of God delayed, it is nevertheless sure, and the day is fast approaching when an awful destruction of self-enthroned beings will be executed. . . . It would seem that Satan cherishes the expectation of accomplishing his purpose until near the end of his career (Rev. 12:7-12).[3]

Perhaps the clearest light upon the fact that Satan has not yet been bound and cast into the lake of fire is found in Matthew 13:24-31. In this parable of the tares and wheat, the Master said,

Allow both to grow together until the harvest; and in the time of the harvest I will say to the reapers, "First gather up the tares and bind them in bundles to burn them up; but gather the wheat into my barn." [13:30]

We may not be able to understand God's strategy, but faith can affirm, "As for God, His way is perfect."

But the time of harvest is fast approaching when the sentence will be executed. We have already noticed the doom of the beast and the false prophet, both of whom were cast alive into the lake of fire (Revelation 19:20).

In Revelation 20:2-3, John sees "the dragon, the serpent of old, who is the devil and Satan," seized and bound for a thousand years and thrown into the pit, so that his nefarious activities would be curtailed.

H. B. Swete's suggested explanation of the temporary loosing of Satan is that in a period of peace and righteousness, in a time when there was no opposition, people might easily come to take their faith too lightly and as a matter of course. The loosing of the devil would be a time to test believers, when the reality of their faith would be demonstrated.[4]

The execution of the deferred sentence on the devil is

compassed in very few words. When he leads his last attack against the people of God, his hosts will be decimated. "Fire came down from heaven and devoured them" (Revelation 20:9).

And what of their leader? "The devil who deceived them was thrown into the lake of fire and brimstone, where the beast and the false prophet are also; and they will be tormented day and night forever and ever" (Revelation 20:10).

> He shall reign o'er all the earth,
> He who wore the crown of thorn,
> Whom they deemed of little worth,
> Whom they met with shame and scorn.
>   Send the tidings forth that all
>   Humbly at His feet may fall.
>   S. G. Stock

Notes

CHAPTER 1

1. F. J. Huegel, *That Old Serpent the Devil* (London: Marshall, Morgan, and Scott, n.d.), p. 14.
2. Edgar Brightman, quoted in ibid., p. 39.
3. J. I. Packer, source unknown.
4. Alan Richardson, *Dictionary of Theology* (London: SCM, 1969), p. 304.
5. Owen C. Whitehouse, in *A Dictionary of the Bible,* ed. James Hastings (Edinburgh: T. & T. Clarke, 1911), S. V. Demon, Devil.
6. A. T. Pierson, *The Bible and Spiritual Life* (New York: Gospel Publ., 1908), p. 162.
7. Maldwyn Hughes, source unknown.
8. Denis de Rougemont, *La Part du Diable,* as quoted in D. G. Barnhouse, *The Invisible War* (Grand Rapids: Zondervan, 1965), p. 156.

CHAPTER 2

1. F. C. Jennings, *Satan: His Person, Work, Place, and Destiny* (New York: Gaebelein, n.d.), p. 58.

CHAPTER 3

1. F. C. Jennings, *Satan,* p. 66.
2. William Hendriksen, *Epistle to the Ephesians* (Grand Rapids: Baker, 1966), p. 113.

CHAPTER 4

1. L. S. Chafer, *Satan* (New York: Gospel Publ., 1922), p. 16.
2. W. H. Griffith Thomas, *Genesis* (Chicago: Moody, n.d.), p. 46.

CHAPTER 5

1. A. T. Pierson, *The Bible and Spiritual Life,* p. 170.
2. *The Scofield Bible* (New York: Oxford, U., 1945), p. 1342.

CHAPTER 6

1. A. T. Pierson, *The Bible and Spiritual Life,* p. 172.

2. L. L. Morris, source unknown.

CHAPTER 7

1. D. G. Barnhouse, *The Invisible War* (Grand Rapids: Zondervan, 1965), p. 156.
2. C. S. Lewis, *Screwtape Letters* (London: G. Bles, 1942), p. 9.
3. Mildred Cable, *Ambassadors for Christ* (London: Hodder & Stoughton, 1935), p. 74.
4. Barnhouse, p. 170.

CHAPTER 8

1. F. C. Jennings, *Satan,* p. 152.

CHAPTER 9

1. F. J. Huegel, *The Enthroned Life* (London: Overcomer Trust, n.d.), pp. 35-36.
2. Quoted by Mrs. F. Howard Taylor, *Behind the Ranges* (London: Lutterworth, 1944), p. 91.
3. Tertullian *Apology.*
4. Quoted by Taylor, p. 114.

CHAPTER 10

1. D. G. Barnhouse, *The Invisible War,* p. 226.
2. F. C. Jennings, *Satan,* p. 77.
3. Harold J. Ockenga, *The Epistle to the Thessalonians,* Proclaiming the New Testament No. 10 (Grand Rapids: Baker, 1962), p. 114.

CHAPTER 11

1. E. M. Bounds, *Satan, His Personality, Power, and Overthrow* (Grand Rapids: Baker, 1963), p. 143.

CHAPTER 12

1. M. F. Unger, *Biblical Demonology* (Wheaton, Ill.: Scripture Press, 1952), p. 79.
2. James L. Wilson, *Principles of War* (Annapolis: Christian Books, 1964), p. 29.
3. A. T. Pierson, *The Bible and Spiritual Life,* p. 189.

CHAPTER 13

1. C. S. Lovett, *Dealing with the Devil* (Personal Christianity, 1967), p. 82-83.
2. D. G. Barnhouse, *The Invisible War,* p. 184.
3. L. S. Chafer, *Satan,* p. 20.
4. H. B. Swete, source unknown.